Praise for Saints Around the World

"Accessible, fascinating, and COOL! Every parent, teacher, and catechist should immediately order copies of *Saints Around The World* by Meg Hunter-Kilmer and Lindsey Sanders. This eclectic sampling of Saints, many of whom you may have never heard of before, shows incredible diversity across cultures and backgrounds and gives us enlightening history and geography lessons, as well as moving examples of how mere humans, regular people like us, became saints by remaining true to God's design for their lives. We can make the world a better place and have the joy of Christ's love no matter what our circumstances. My children, aged seven to sixteen, were transfixed by the stunning artwork and captivated by the beautifully written biographical details. These intriguing stories are not about make-believe characters, but about real people who are now in heaven and can be powerful intercessors for us. Real heroes that can be our spiritual friends and confidantes, helping us to cope with our fears and anxieties and inspiring us with their bravery and love of God."

JEANNIE GAFFIGAN, Producer, Writer, Philanthropist, Mother of Five, and *New York Times* Bestselling Author of *When Life Gives You Pears*

"If you own only one Saints book—for your kids OR yourself—own this one. Meg Hunter-Kilmer and Lindsey Sanders have produced a book that is a joy, a delight, a beauty, a wellspring of inspiring stories, and a sure help on the path to sainthood for your whole family. It's a true treasure."

EMILY STIMPSON CHAPMAN, Author of *The Catholic Table*

"God created each and every single one of us for no other reason than because He wants for us to become saints. Unfortunately, most of us grow up in churches that only depict some members of the body of Christ as holy. If we don't encounter saints who look like us or have stories similar to our own then we might grow up thinking that becoming a saint is not an option for us. Representation matters. Meg Hunter-Kilmer's book, *Saints Around the World* makes up for what is lacking in many of our churches. I believe that the stories and images of the Saints depicted in this work will inspire a whole new generation of saints from every race, nation, tribe, and tongue."

FR. JOSH JOHNSON, Director of Vocations for the Diocese of Baton Rouge, Pastor of Our Lady of the Holy Rosary, Author of *Broken & Blessed*, and Host of the "Ask Fr. Josh" Podcast

"The majesty of God is mirrored in the diversity of His saints. I can't wait to read this book to my daughter so she knows them and Him better."

LEAH LIBRESCO SARGEANT, Author of *Arriving at Amen* and *Building the Benedict Option*

"Meg has done the incredible: she has made the Catholic Saints that we know and love (and many that we are just meeting for the first time) more accessible, warm, human, and well . . . just like us! Coupled with the beautiful art from Lindsey Sanders showing the diversity of God's wondrous creation, Meg reminds us all that we are called to sainthood . . . no matter the bumps in the road we experience along the way."

KARIANNA FREY, Educator, Speaker, and Author of *The Virtuous Path: A Daily Examination of Conscience Journal for Kids*

"Growing up Hindu in a small, somewhat rural town, even after my conversion, it never dawned on me that there were Saints of the Church who resembled my own family. With this incredible new book from Meg Hunter-Kilmer, illustrated so stunningly by Lindsey Sanders, my children can grow up knowing that the family of God resembles their own diverse family in every way, and in every generation. Written in a first-person narrative, we can get to know these Saints from around the world with the intimacy of a real-life friend, here and now. What a gift this collection of stories is! Truth be told, while it will be read to my children, I want to keep a copy for myself as well."

RAKHI MCCORMICK, Owner, Creative, and Writer at Rakstar Designs

"What joy for the universal Church to have diverse Saints from all ages, stages, and walks of life—and what a gift for our children to celebrate the inspiration of women, men, and children who give such strong examples of faith! *Saints Around the World* is a lively and vivid introduction to Saints and Blesseds throughout history and around the globe. As we encourage children to follow God's unique call for their lives, what better companions for their journey than the holy people who have served God and others in both ordinary and unforgettable ways? Meg Hunter-Kilmer and Lindsey Sanders have created a treasure with this collection that will help families to pray and learn together for years to come."

LAURA KELLY FANUCCI, Author of *Everyday Sacrament: The Messy Grace of Parenting*

"This book is a joy to read. You'll be meeting a lot of new heavenly friends and intercessors for the first time, and learning an essential lesson in the process: no matter when or where you're from, there's no reason not to become a saint yourself!"

FR. CASSIDY STINSON, Priest of the Diocese of Richmond

"What Bl. Carlo Acutis did in bringing Eucharistic miracles to our attention through a compilation of stories, people, places, and events, Meg Hunter-Kilmer is doing with the Saints! Her research and relatable reflections, accompanied by the beautiful watercolor artwork of Lindsey Sanders, make learning about and praying with the Blesseds and Saints a joyful glimpse of Heaven while also being grounded by their humanity on earth. Meg brings to light the God-given diversity of cultures, abilities, temperaments, ages, and backgrounds of each person and shows us that, no matter our circumstances, it's never too early or too late to say 'Yes!' To Jesus."

CHIKA ANYANWU, Catholic Speaker, For Greater Things Ministry

"With captivating storytelling and warm, richly detailed illustrations, *Saints Around the World* shows a glimpse of the beautiful uniqueness that is the universal call to holiness, sharing Saints from all eras, locations, and backgrounds. Among these pages, children will find one hundred holy friends and discover new patrons and prayer warriors, but most importantly will hear the call that *they* are created to be saints, too! The great care and intentionality given to each inch of this book make it a timeless resource for kids of all ages."

KATIE BOGNER, Teacher, DRE, and Author of
Through the Year with Jesus: Gospel Readings and Reflections for Children

"I love this book. It is captivating and engaging, and my squirmy 3-year-old loves to look at the pictures, listen to the stories, and then name her baby dolls after the Saints she's just met. Get this book. Get two copies. Because you may not want to share with your kids."

KATIE PREJEAN MCGRADY, Speaker, Author, and Podcast Host

"If you are a parent, grandparent, godparent, or know a child, you are going to want to get them this book. I think of myself as someone who is familiar with the Saints, but there are so many amazing lesser-known Saints included in this treasury of holy men and women that I had never heard of before! I guarantee that you and the children in your life will find new friends in heaven while reading these pages, too."

HALEY STEWART, Author of *The Grace of Enough*

SAINTS
Around the World

SAINTS
Around the World

Meg Hunter-Kilmer

Illustrated by Lindsey Sanders

EMMAUS
ROAD
PUBLISHING

Emmaus Road Publishing
1468 Parkview Circle
Steubenville, Ohio 43952
EmmausRoad.org

Library of Congress Control Number: 2021933682
978-1-64585-115-8 hardcover | 978-1-64585-116-5 ebook

Cover design and layout by Patty Borgman

To the Hill children, whose delight in these Saints and their pictures (and their indices) fills my heart. May your lives give as much glory to God as theirs.
—*M.H.-K.*

To Mary Most Fruitful, and to my kids, who gave me a reason to paint.
—*L.S.*

"I will make you a light to the nations, that my salvation may reach to the ends of the earth."
—Isaiah 49:6

FOR MAP KEY, see the numbers next to
the Saint names in the Table of Contents.

Table of Contents

Dear Reader,

Did you know that for ever and always, since before he even made the universe, God has been hoping that you would be a saint?

Really and truly!

It's the whole reason he came to earth and became a baby, the whole reason he was a little boy and grew to be a kind and strong and interesting and wonderful man. And it's the whole reason he died on the Cross and rose on the third day—because he wanted so badly for you to be in heaven with him.

Lots of people think that only old people can be saints, or only healthy people or clever people or successful people or boring people or people who look a certain way or talk a certain way or act a certain way. But that's just not true! There are Saints and Blesseds* in our Church from all over the world, from little kids to old men, from beggars to queens and everything in between.

Some of them were really big sinners before they met Jesus. Some of them were really big sinners even after they met Jesus. Some of them lived very ordinary lives and some of them had wild adventures. Some of them were geniuses and some of them weren't clever at all. Some had disabilities and some had tempers and some had families who were really hard to be around. In this book, you'll meet all kinds of Saints.

And when you begin to get to know them, I think you'll see that God is calling every kind of person to be a saint. Even if you're little or quiet or really interested in stuff that has nothing to do with church or always messing up no matter how hard you try.

I hope that in these pages you will find Saints and Blesseds who make you say, "Wow! She's a lot like me!" Or, "Wow! I want to be like him!" Or maybe, "Wow! I didn't know people like that could be Saints!"

But there's one thing I know you won't find here: a Saint who is just exactly like you.

That's because you're the only you there has ever been. The only you there ever will be. God has been hoping to make you a saint exactly as you are. And the world needs a saint who is just like you.

The Saints go before us to show us that it's possible, that God really can make us holy, can make our lives wonderful and glorious. And they pray for us, asking God to pour out his graces on us so that we can become

---

* *A saint (with a little s) is anybody at all who's in heaven, even if nobody on earth knows it. A Saint (with a big S) is somebody who the Church has declared to be in heaven and invited everybody to honor. And a Blessed is somebody whom we can confidently believe to be in heaven even though the Church hasn't yet invited absolutely everybody to honor him or her.*

holy. Isn't it marvelous that we have this whole big wonderful family in heaven? Let's start getting to know them!

You can begin reading, or flip to a picture that looks interesting and start there. Or go to the back of the book, where you'll see Saints listed by country, feast day, or gifts and struggles. There is a guide to help you sound out the harder names. But don't worry if you can't figure one out—just do the best you can. And if you want to learn more about the pictures in the book, there's a note from the illustrator, Lindsey Sanders, for each one, telling you why you see a certain hat or tree or building or hand gesture. Once you start reading her notes, you'll discover that there's a lot more going on in the pictures than you realized!

Most importantly, remember: these are real people who really lived and are really alive in Jesus. They want to be your friends, to pray for you, and to show you how to love God better. When you find Saints or Blesseds who you really like, stop to ask them to pray for you. It's such a wonderful thing to have intercessors in heaven.

In the Love of Jesus,

Meg Hunter-Kilmer

Author Meg (with her ever-present Bible)
and illustrator Lindsey (with her ever-present babies)

St. Adelaide of Burgundy

AD-uh-LADE of Burgundy
Switzerland, Germany | 931–999
Feast Day: December 16

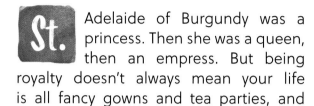 Adelaide of Burgundy was a princess. Then she was a queen, then an empress. But being royalty doesn't always mean your life is all fancy gowns and tea parties, and Adelaide's life was anything but easy.

Adelaide was married when she was sixteen, which was quite grown-up then, and soon she was the queen of Italy. But she had only been queen for two years when her husband, the king, was poisoned by an enemy who wanted to steal his throne. Then, that same villain Berengar tried to make Adelaide marry his son.

Adelaide refused. Even when Berengar hurt her. Even when he threw her in a dungeon.

But Adelaide, who still wasn't even twenty years old, was not going to sit by and languish in a dungeon while her kingdom was being ruined by a murderer. She escaped through a tunnel, journeyed through a swamp, and arrived at a fortress, where she sent a message to King Otto of Germany, asking him to join with her to defeat Berengar. King Otto rode to meet the widowed queen and escort her to safety. When he saw her courage and wisdom and holiness and beauty, he asked her to be his queen. The scary part of Adelaide's life was over.

But that didn't mean things were easy. She had to help her husband rule, then her son after him. And ruling an empire was a tough job. Then, when Adelaide was almost fifty, her son's wife demanded that Adelaide be sent away. A woman as powerful and clever as Adelaide could have fought back, but Adelaide was perfectly happy to be done being an empress. She began to do the work she was really interested in: building churches and monasteries, serving the poor, and preaching the Gospel. She'd had quite enough of wild adventures and power and plots. Now, Adelaide just wanted to pray.

That's what she did for the rest of her life (with a few years off to help her grandson run the empire). Adelaide's life hadn't been easy. But in the end, it wasn't being a warrior queen that had made her a Saint. St. Adelaide of Burgundy is a Saint because she gave her heart to Jesus and her life to his people, and you don't have to be a princess to do that.

St. Adelaide is standing in an archway at Memleben Abbey, an abbey built by her son, Otto II, in the town where her husband, Otto I, died. Because she ruled as regent for her grandson, she's holding the orb and scepter that symbolize power over the Holy Roman Empire.

St. Agatha Kim A-gi

AG-ah-tha KIM ah-GHEE
South Korea | 1787–1839
Feast Day: May 24

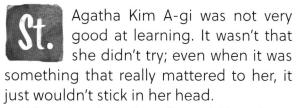 Agatha Kim A-gi was not very good at learning. It wasn't that she didn't try; even when it was something that really mattered to her, it just wouldn't stick in her head.

When Agatha's sister first told her about Jesus, Agatha was thrilled to hear the story of the Son of God who died and rose for her! Still, when she tried to memorize prayers and doctrines and commandments, Agatha couldn't remember a word.

But you don't have to be clever to be a Saint. And even though Agatha had a really hard time learning, she loved Jesus. She wanted to be baptized.

Before the other Christians would baptize her, though, they asked Agatha to recite the Creed. "I only know Jesus and Mary," she said. Could she pray the Our Father? "I only know Jesus and Mary." What about the Hail Mary? "I only know Jesus and Mary."

So they told her she wasn't smart enough to be baptized.

Now you and I know that's not true. Baptism is a free gift from the God who loves us and nobody who wants to belong to Jesus is left out. But the Church in Korea was very new, and for years they hadn't had any priests in the whole country, just some holy people who were doing the best they could. And sometimes holy people doing the best they can get things wrong.

When they told her she couldn't be baptized, Agatha must have felt just awful. But the government didn't care that Agatha wasn't baptized. They knew she loved Jesus and arrested her all the same. When they asked her to deny Jesus, there was just one answer Agatha could give:

"I only know Jesus and Mary."

That's what she said when they asked her to betray her friends, too. "I only know Jesus and Mary." When they hit her and hurt her, she only said, "Jesus! Mary!" And when she was taken to prison, the Christians there bowed before her and said, "Here is Agatha, who only knows Jesus and Mary."

Agatha's great shame had become her crowning glory. They baptized her, and when she died a martyr, nobody asked her to recite Bible verses or define tricky words. All that mattered was that St. Agatha Kim A-gi loved Jesus and Mary, and they loved her.

St. Agatha is dressed in a traditional hanbok. Though she would likely have worn white on ordinary occasions, we put her in pink to show that her martyrdom would have been a joyous event. She's standing in her prison cell, the bars made of bamboo, with a bucket of water to show that she was baptized in prison.

St. Albert Chmielowski

AL-behrt shmeh-LOF-skee (*more accurately, hmyeh-LOF-skee*)
Poland | 1845–1916
Feast Day: December 25

 Albert Chmielowski was full of surprises. When he was an eighteen-year-old soldier fighting for Polish independence and was shot in the leg, enemy soldiers discovered Albert and told him his injured leg would have to be amputated with no medicine to take the pain away. They didn't expect him to be so brave, but Albert just said, "Give me a cigar." And he smoked that cigar to pass the time while they cut off his leg!

After his amputation, they took him to a hospital. They should have known that Albert was no average teenager. But they sure didn't expect him to sneak out of their hospital in a coffin and escape to Belgium. And when he got there, I bet nobody expected the tough-as-nails soldier with a wooden leg to learn to paint. But that's just what Albert did, becoming a painter whose art was famous all over Europe. Eventually, he returned home and became friends with the most important artists and actors and writers in Poland.

But Albert wasn't happy. Once, he was so sad he even had to go to the hospital. The doctors helped him a lot, but Albert's life needed to change, too. He had money and fame and friends, but he still felt empty. So he began searching for God's will, and soon he founded an order of Franciscan friars.

Well, nobody expected that! If Albert had been surprising before, now he was shocking. To leave behind the amazing life he'd built for himself, a life envied by all of Poland? It didn't make sense.

But Br. Albert had seen the suffering of the poor, and he couldn't ignore it. He sold his paintings and spent his life working to serve the poor with the people who joined him. And he became so holy that many years later a young poet and playwright named Karol Wojtyła looked at Br. Albert's example and left behind the world of art to become a priest. He went on to be elected pope and canonized: St. John Paul II.

St. Albert Chmielowski's life is a witness not just to artists but to everybody that God can use every bit of us, that following the Lord will lead to a life full of wonderful surprises, and that life in Jesus is always, always more beautiful than without him.

St. Albert is dressed in his Franciscan habit, his prosthetic leg visible beneath his tunic. He's shown turning from his life as an artist to his life in service to the poor. All the paintings on the wall are Br. Albert's work; the most famous is the Ecce Homo, the painting of Jesus to Br. Albert's right.

St. Alphonsa Muttathupadathu

al-FON-sah
MOOH-tah-thooh-PAH-da-thooh
India | 1910–1946
Feast Day: July 28

Alphonsa Muttathupadathu was usually sick. When she was only three, she got a skin infection that lasted for almost a year and nearly killed her. When she was a teenager, she fell into a fire pit and burned her feet so badly she was disabled for the rest of her life. Soon after she entered the convent, she got sores all over her legs and a terrible nosebleed. After that was cured, she got pneumonia.

And that wasn't all. Alphonsa's mother had died when she was just a baby, and the aunt who raised her wasn't very kind to her. Her family tried to force her to get married when she knew God was calling her to be a Syro-Malabar Sister. And one time someone broke into her room at the convent and scared her so badly she got amnesia, forgot how to read and write, and became so sick for so long that everyone thought she was going to die. She got better after receiving Anointing of the Sick, but was never really well again.

It would have been really easy for Sr. Alphonsa to be bitter about all that. It would have been even easier for her to feel ashamed, to think she was a burden and her illnesses and disability meant she was worthless. She couldn't teach most of the time, which was what she was supposed to do, and a lot of her life was spent in bed, needing other people to take care of her.

But Sr. Alphonsa knew something very important: God loved her. Really, it's the most important thing a person can know. And because she knew that, Sr. Alphonsa knew that it didn't matter what she could do or offer; she was loved. She wasn't a burden: she was a child of God and a bride of Christ. Whatever her disability or illness or suffering, God would never, never stop loving her.

Alphonsa knew this when she was a little girl and she knew it when she was a Sister. So when she suffered, she still trusted God. And she loved him back. No matter how hard things got, St. Alphonsa Muttathupadathu never stopped loving God or trusting him. And that's what made her a Saint.

St. Alphonsa is wearing her Franciscan Clarist habit. To her right is a large stone cross, one of the St. Thomas crosses that have been found all over Christian India for many centuries. The peacock is the national bird of India and a symbol of St. Thomas, who was (according to legend) killed in India by a man hunting peacocks. Peacocks are often found on the stone crosses of India.

Bl. Ana of the Angels Monteagudo

AH-nah of the Angels
MOHN-tay-ah-GOO-doh
Peru | 1602–1686
Feast Day: January 10

Plenty of Saints were attacked by the enemies of the Church. But some were attacked by enemies within the Church, by priests and nuns who hated them for their holiness. That's what happened to Bl. Ana of the Angels Monteagudo.

Ana's father was a wealthy Spaniard and her mother was the daughter of an Incan princess. They sent Ana to a convent boarding school, hoping she would learn to be a good wife as well as a good Christian, but Ana knew she was called to be a nun. When her parents brought her home so she could marry a nice boy they'd picked out, they were not pleased to hear about her vocation.

So, like so many Saints before her, Ana ran away to become a nun. Well, her parents marched straight over to that convent and demanded that she come home.

Ana refused.

Her father offered her gold and jewels.

Ana refused.

Then her mother made a threat: "If you stay today, don't you ever try to come home again." Ana gasped, then nodded. If she had to lose her family to be with Jesus, so be it.

Sr. Ana was a very holy nun. She prophesied and worked miracles and even had visions of Mary and the angels asking her to pray for the souls in purgatory. But the other nuns didn't want to be holy. They wanted to do what they liked and eat what they liked and pray when they liked, which wasn't very often. And when Sr. Ana was put in charge of them, they made fun of her. Sr. Ana didn't know how to read or write, and the other Sisters used to laugh at her. Can you imagine?

Well, that was bad enough. But when Sr. Ana started to make them follow the rules, it got worse. They tried to poison her! Three times! If it were me, I might have given up on being a nun. Or at least started a new convent without murderers in it! But Sr. Ana wanted to help her Sisters become saints, so she stayed. And, little by little, over many years, it worked. By her prayers and her witness, Bl. Ana of the Angels led her Sisters to holiness—even the ones who fought her.

Bl. Ana is wearing her Dominican habit and standing by an angry letter from her mother and the heaps of treasure her parents offered if she would leave the convent. A cup with a snake generally symbolizes poison; this one is a reminder of the three times Sr. Ana's Sisters tried to poison her. The angels beside her are the ones who appeared to her, asking her to pray for the holy souls in purgatory.

St. André Bessette

AHN-dray buh-SET
Canada | 1845–1937
Feast Day: January 6

André Bessette didn't look like he had much to offer. He was weak and usually sick. He couldn't read or write. He was bad at every job he tried: farming, shoemaking, blacksmithing, and baking. When he tried to enter the Holy Cross Brothers, even they didn't want him. But the bishop of Montreal had a feeling that André was a Saint in the making. After he talked to the Brothers, they didn't have much choice but to let André in.

Still, his superiors had no idea what to do with him. He certainly couldn't teach, and he'd already proven that he wasn't any good with his hands. So they sent Br. André to answer the door. Surely he couldn't get into any trouble there, could he?

I suppose it depends on what you mean by trouble. Br. André did a great job—such a great job it became a problem. You see, people would come to the door to ask for prayers, and Br. André would pray with them. And, again and again, there would be a miracle. So more people started to come, and more, and more. And people who couldn't make the trip started to write letters. Before long, the weak little Brother (who everyone thought was useless) was getting eighty-thousand letters a year and needed four secretaries to help answer them.

But Br. André insisted it had nothing to do with him. "I just tell St. Joseph," he said. "He's the one who cures people." Br. André really loved St. Joseph. He wanted to build a shrine to St. Joseph, so he began collecting donations of nickels and pennies. Soon he had enough for a small chapel—then a larger one, and larger still. The Oratory of St. Joseph that stands there now is the biggest church in Canada. It's full of crutches and wheelchairs, left behind by people who didn't need them after being healed. At least sixty thousand people were healed during Br. André's lifetime, and the miracles continue today.

When the sickly (and seemingly useless) Brother died at ninety-one, a million people came to pay their respects. They understood what his superiors hadn't: Br. André didn't need to be strong or clever or talented. By little, ordinary acts of faithfulness, St. André Bessette had become a miracle-worker and a Saint.

St. André is wearing his Holy Cross habit and holding open the door to the Oratory of St. Joseph, the church he built through people's donations of pennies (held in the jar at his feet). He died before the Oratory was completed, but in the background you see the church as it stands today. The bronze statue of St. Joseph was erected in Br. André's time and stands nearly ten feet tall atop a twenty-foot pedestal.

St. Augustine Phan Viết Huy, St. Dominic Đinh Đạt, & St. Nicholas Bùi Đức Thể

uh-GUS-tin fahn viet hooie, Dominic din dat, Nicholas booie dook tay (*booie as in buoy, dook rhyming with book*)
Vietnam | 1795–1839, 1803–1839, 1792–1839
Feast Day: November 24

 How far would you go to make something right? That was the question Sts. Augustine Phan Viết Huy, Dominic Đinh Đạt, and Nicholas Bùi Đức Thể had to ask themselves after they denied Jesus.

The governor of their province didn't want his soldiers to be Christians. When he told them that, most of the five hundred Christian soldiers denied Jesus right there, but not Augustine, Dominic, and Nicholas. Soon, they were the only men left who refused to stomp on a crucifix. For months their captors hit them and hurt them, but the three Christian soldiers remained strong.

The emperor of Vietnam didn't want these prisoners killed, he wanted their faith broken. So the governor tried something new. He took one of Nicholas' friends and threatened to hurt him, instead.

This was finally too much. After months of suffering, Nicholas couldn't stand to see someone else being made to suffer. So he stomped on Jesus. Augustine and Dominic did, too, and were given their freedom.

But they felt just terrible about what they'd done. After all those months, they'd betrayed Jesus. They went straight to find a priest in hiding to hear their Confessions.

But the three courageous men weren't satisfied. They knew their sin had been taken away by God's mercy, but they didn't want people to hear about them and think it was okay to deny Jesus. They had to fix this. So they marched right back to the governor and declared that they loved Jesus more than ever.

But the governor had already told the emperor about their apostasy and he didn't want to look like a failure. So he sent the men home and told them not to say anything. Augustine, Dominic, and Nicholas weren't happy with that. They wanted to make this right. So they decided they would go all the way to the emperor and tell him that they were Christians. Can you imagine the courage that took? But they were so dreadfully sorry for what they'd done that they didn't mind at all. In the end, the emperor had them killed. But Sts. Augustine Phan Viết Huy, Dominic Đinh Đạt, and Nicholas Bùi Đức Thể died with smiles on their faces, knowing that God had given them the grace to make things right.

St. Augustine stands between Sts. Dominic (left) and Nicholas (right). He was the last of the three to stomp on the cross and the first to insist that they go to the emperor. As the leader of the group, he holds a sword to show that he was a true soldier of Christ. All three hold palms (the symbol of martyrs' victory) and are dressed in the uniform worn by soldiers in Emperor Minh Mang's army.

St. Augustine Yu Chin-gil & St. Peter Yu Tae-chol

uh-GUS-tin YOO chin-GHIL,
Peter YOO tay-CHOHL
South Korea | 1791–1839, 1826–1839
Feast Day: September 20

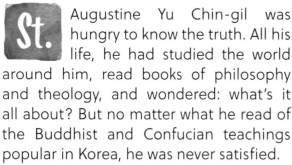 Augustine Yu Chin-gil was hungry to know the truth. All his life, he had studied the world around him, read books of philosophy and theology, and wondered: what's it all about? But no matter what he read of the Buddhist and Confucian teachings popular in Korea, he was never satisfied.

Then one day, Augustine opened an old chest and saw writing inside: a scrap of paper that had been used to repair the chest. He scraped the bits of paper off and pieced them together to reveal a forbidden book. It told all about the God who had created the world, come into it as a human baby, died to save all people, and risen from the dead. Suddenly Augustine understood. This was what life was all about! This was the meaning he was looking for: to love God and be loved by him.

But it was illegal to be a Catholic, so Augustine had to be very careful when he asked around to find out more. Eventually, he found some other secret Christians who could answer his questions, but there wasn't a single priest in the country, and there hadn't been for twenty-five years. Augustine waited and longed and hoped and finally snuck into China with his friend St. Paul Chong Ha-sang and was baptized at last.

When Augustine returned home, he found that he had even more reason to rejoice: he had a brand new son! He named the boy Peter Yu Tae-chol and raised him as a Christian even though the rest of his family didn't believe in Jesus. For thirteen years, Augustine helped lead the Church in Korea. He wrote to the pope asking him to send priests to Korea and snuck around the country telling people about how much God loved them, though he never could convince his wife and daughters.

He sure did convince his son, though. When Augustine was arrested for being a Christian, thirteen-year-old Peter went straight to the authorities and told them that he was a Christian, too, and ready to die with his dad. St. Augustine Yu Chin-gil and St. Peter Yu Tae-chol were both martyred. A bit of trash had led them to the greatest treasure in this world or the next.

Sts. Augustine and Peter are shown in traditional Korean dress. Augustine's hat is a samo, worn by government officials, and Peter's is a bokkeon, worn by boys. Augustine is carrying the letter that he and St. Paul Chong Ha-sang wrote to the pope to request that missionary priests be sent to Korea. Behind them are the hills of Korea and the leaves of a Korean maple tree.

St. Barnabas

BAR-na-bus
Cyprus | d. 61
Feast Day: June 11

St. Barnabas was a really good friend. When St. Paul tried to tell the Christians that he had met Jesus, nobody believed him. Paul had persecuted them, after all, so when he showed up saying that he was a Christian, people were suspicious and afraid.

I guess they had forgotten that loving Jesus can change you. Maybe Matthew didn't remember how he used to be a tax collector and Peter didn't remember that he'd denied Jesus. But Barnabas remembered. He remembered how big grace is and he remembered how powerful God is. So he took a risk: he went to talk to Paul.

Isn't it a good thing he did? Paul became one of the most important Saints ever, but Barnabas made it possible. They became a team, traveling all around the Mediterranean preaching.

Thousands of people were baptized! But plenty of others were not. They ignored Paul and Barnabas. They ran them out of town. Sometimes they worshipped them as gods and sometimes they stoned them as demons. It must have been exhausting.

Paul can't always have been easy to be around, either. In his letters we see that he had big feelings and a short temper. But Barnabas didn't give up on him. Paul was his friend and the two of them had work to do for Jesus.

Barnabas wasn't just loyal to Paul, though. He was loyal to all his friends. And when Paul didn't want Barnabas' cousin Mark to travel with them, Barnabas put his foot down. Mark had abandoned them once, but he had said that he was sorry and that he wouldn't do it again. Barnabas trusted him, just like he had trusted Paul so long before. Paul didn't. So Barnabas and Paul separated.

We don't know exactly what happened between them after that, but we know that Paul forgave Mark and asked him to come back and work with him. So probably he and Barnabas made up, too. But even if they never saw each other again, they never stopped loving each other. Imagine how wonderful it was when they were reunited in heaven after all those years! But not nearly as wonderful as seeing Jesus. Because as good a friend as St. Barnabas was to St. Paul, he was an even better friend to Jesus. And that's what made him a Saint.

St. Barnabas was the apostle to Cyprus; his appearance here is reminiscent of the flag of Cyprus, which is white and orange with olive branches. One of Barnabas' symbols is the olive branch, showing his nature as a peacemaker, particularly between Saul (Paul) and the rest of the Christian community. The boat behind him reminds us of his many travels by sea to preach the Gospel.

Bl. Benedetta Bianchi Porro

BEN-uh-DET-ah bee-ON-kee POR-roh
Italy | 1936–1964
Feast Day: January 23

Bl. Benedetta Bianchi Porro was going deaf, and nobody believed her. They made fun of her when she couldn't understand them, and even though she learned to read their lips, they failed her in exams when she couldn't hear the questions.

Benedetta knew what it was like to be made fun of for a disability. She'd had polio when she was a baby, which left her right leg shorter than her left and meant she had to wear a painful back brace to keep her spine straight. But even though she was used to being teased and taunted, not being believed was awfully hard.

Still, Benedetta knew what was happening. She was in school to be a doctor, so she began to do the research that doctors wouldn't do for her. She discovered that she had a terrible disease that would make her go deaf and blind and even make her lose her sense of taste and smell. Eventually, she wouldn't be able to move at all.

Benedetta was tempted to lose hope. It was hard not to give up on God when it felt like he had given up on her. She got sicker and sicker. She had to leave medical school only a year before she would have become a doctor. But God was working in her heart, and instead of becoming more miserable, Benedetta found more and more joy.

She was still afraid sometimes. She still felt alone sometimes. But even when Benedetta wanted to cry out in sorrow, she knew that Jesus was bringing her deeper and deeper into his Sacred Heart. She trusted God, even when she didn't feel it.

In the end, Benedetta couldn't see or hear. People could only talk to her by spelling in sign language on her cheek. She was totally paralyzed except for her left hand. But Benedetta could speak, and she told people of the goodness of God, his beautiful love, and the longing she had for heaven.

"I do not lack hope," Benedetta said. "I know that at the end of the road, Jesus is waiting for me. . . . My days are not easy. They are hard. But sweet because Jesus is with me." In silence and darkness and stillness and loneliness, Bl. Benedetta Bianchi Porro had found that God is still good. Always, always, always.

Bl. Benedetta was a fashionable young woman, with stylish clothes and hair in nearly all her pictures. Though she's blind in this picture, she's profoundly aware of the light of Christ at work in her life. Through all her struggles, Benedetta clung to the Cross. Once, when a friend brought her a crucifix, she touched it and said, "I, too, must be like this, but always joyfully."

Bl. Benedict Daswa

BEN-uh-dict das-WAH
South Africa | 1946–1990
Feast Day: February 1

It's awfully easy to care too much about what other people think. And when we do, sometimes we find ourselves doing things we never wanted to do, just so people won't make fun of us.

Bl. Benedict Daswa didn't have that problem. He did the right thing his whole life. Even when people made fun of him. Even when they killed him.

Benedict was born in a small village in South Africa. His family wasn't Christian, but when Benedict was a teenager, he met a Catholic man and learned about Jesus for the first time. After hearing how God loved him and died for him, Benedict knew he had to become Catholic. It wasn't easy in a village where almost nobody was Catholic yet, but Benedict always did what he knew was right.

When he grew up, Benedict became a teacher, a soccer coach, and eventually a school principal. He got married and had eight children. He was a pretty ordinary dad.

Benedict also cooked and changed diapers. He did laundry and worked in the garden. He hugged his kids. That probably also sounds like ordinary dad stuff to you, but some people in Benedict's village thought only women should do those things.

Do you think Benedict cared? Of course not! He loved his wife and he loved his kids and he wanted to serve them, whatever other people thought.

Benedict had bigger problems than just people saying ugly things about him, though. Many of his people believed in witchcraft. They asked witches to help them and they blamed witches when things went wrong. And when they tried to make him give them money to find and kill a witch, Benedict refused. It was only about two dollars, but he knew it was wrong to kill people and he wasn't willing to do evil just to make other people happy.

It didn't just make them unhappy, though. It made them furious. They ambushed Benedict and killed him. And while his wife and his children were very, very sad, they were also very, very proud of how good and brave he had been. His whole life, Bl. Benedict Daswa had done what was right, no matter what other people said or did, and that made him a hero.

Bl. Benedict is holding one of his children in one arm and a soccer ball in the other. He's wearing a tie, which he called "the rope of honor" and required of all his male teachers. He's surrounded by fruit trees: bananas, mangoes, and oranges, all of which he grew so successfully that people actually accused him of using witchcraft.

Bl. Carlo Acutis

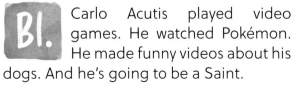

CAR-lo ah-COO-teess
Italy | 1991–2006
Feast Day: October 12

Bl. Carlo Acutis played video games. He watched Pokémon. He made funny videos about his dogs. And he's going to be a Saint.

Carlo's parents didn't take him to church when he was little, but somehow he heard about how Jesus is really present in the Eucharist. Carlo thought that was just amazing. He was only three years old, but he wanted to go visit Jesus whenever he could. And after his First Communion, he went to Mass every day.

Every single day. Even when his mom and dad didn't go with him. Even on vacation. Carlo said he just couldn't understand how thousands of people would line up to go to a concert or a soccer game, but nobody went to visit the God who created them. So he decided to help change that.

Carlo had heard about some Eucharistic miracles. Not just the everyday miracle of how bread is turned into Jesus, but miracles where the Eucharist bleeds or Jesus' face appears on the host. He figured if he told people about these miracles, they would want to go visit Jesus. So Carlo made a website.

You see, Carlo was really good with computers. He knew how to write code and make videos and build websites, and so he made one all about Eucharistic miracles—you can still visit it today! And

he did the whole thing in between riding his bike and practicing saxophone and visiting his friends, especially the ones who were homeless or lonely or bullied. He fit all that in because he was really good at using his time well. He actually had a rule for himself: he would only spend one hour a week playing video games. Can you believe that? But Carlo didn't want to be a slave to screens.

Carlo got very sick very fast and died when he was only fifteen. But he wasn't sad, because he was going home to Jesus. Carlo had always told his friends the first step in being holy: "You have to want it with all your heart." And he really, really did. Bl. Carlo Acutis was an ordinary kid who lived an ordinary life and died an ordinary death, but he's going to be a Saint because in all the ordinary things, he always chose Jesus first.

Bl. Carlo is surrounded by many of his favorite things. To his left is the monstrance that holds the Eucharistic miracle at Lanciano, one of the miracles featured on Carlo's website (www.carloacutis.net) and in his traveling exhibition. His cat Cleopatra and his dog Chiara are beside him. You can also see skis, a Poké Ball, a video camera, a rosary, a bag of leftovers for his homeless friends, his laptop, a soccer ball, and a PlayStation.

Bl. Carlos Manuel Rodríguez Santiago

CAR-lohss mahn-WELL
rode-REE-ghez sahn-tee-AH-go
Puerto Rico | 1918–1963
Feast Day: July 13

Bl. Carlos Manuel Rodríguez Santiago knew that everybody—everybody—is called to be a saint. When he was a little boy, Carlos had wanted to be a priest. He was smart and loved the Mass, so it seemed like just the right thing for him. But when Carlos became sick with ulcerative colitis (a very painful stomach disease), it was hard for him to keep going to school. Eventually, he realized that his illness wasn't ever going to get better, and because of that he was never going to be able to be a priest.

Carlos could have decided that if he couldn't be a priest he would just be mediocre, a not-so-holy Catholic who goes to Mass on Sundays and ignores Jesus the rest of the week. But Carlos knew that you don't have to be a priest or a religious to be holy. So he decided that he was going to become holy in his ordinary lay life, and he was going to help other laypeople become holy, too.

Carlos loved reading and hiking and playing the organ at Mass. But the thing Carlos loved the most was the liturgy—the prayers and rituals of the Church. He knew that the Mass is the most precious thing on earth, and he wanted other people to know that, too. So he began translating the Latin prayers into Spanish so people could understand them. He published a newsletter that shared the prayers of the Mass and articles explaining them (which Carlos translated from Latin or English). He organized groups to study the liturgy and gave talks all about the beauty of the prayers that you and I usually don't even pay attention to.

Carlos worked as an office clerk but lived very simply. He only had one pair of shoes his entire adult life because he used all his money to help people learn about the liturgy. Even though he was sick and usually in pain, he never stopped working to bring other people to Jesus. When Carlos was forty-four, he died of cancer. But he left behind a land filled with ordinary people who loved Jesus so much more because of what Carlos had done. Bl. Carlos Manuel Rodríguez Santiago had known that everyone is called to be a saint, and now they all knew it, too.

Bl. Carlos is standing outside the Sweet Name of Jesus Cathedral in Caguas, Puerto Rico. He's next to the Paschal Candle and holding a candle from the Easter Vigil. The Easter Vigil was his favorite liturgy of the year; he used to say, "We live for this night," and advocated for the Vigil to be moved back to Holy Saturday night after being celebrated in the morning for centuries. In 1951, this was done.

St. Casilda of Toledo

cah-SILL-dah of toh-LAY-do
Spain | 950–1050
Feast Day: April 9

St. Casilda of Toledo had everything a person could possibly want. She was a princess, so she lived in a beautiful palace and wore beautiful clothes and had a mother and father who loved her very much.

But Casilda wasn't happy. Something was missing.

So Casilda began to search. When she saw an enslaved girl in the palace who was always smiling, she asked why. "Even though my life is very hard and often very sad," the girl said, "I know that Jesus loves me so much."

"What do you mean?" Casilda asked. You see, Casilda was Muslim. So even though she knew there was a God, she didn't know that he was her Father who loved her, and she didn't know that Jesus was God who died to save her and rose again. When she heard all this, she was thrilled! She ran right to her daddy the king to tell him all about it. But he wasn't happy at all. In fact, he shouted at her to be silent. It was illegal to be a Christian and he didn't want to have to punish her.

Casilda was heartbroken. But as she trudged out into the courtyard, she heard singing. She followed the sound until she reached a window to the dungeon, where a group of Christians was praising God. Soon Casilda was bringing them food and blankets and listening to all their stories about Jesus.

The more Casilda learned, the more she knew she needed to be a Christian. Without Jesus, she was miserable—so miserable she started to get sick. She got sicker and sicker until her poor daddy was near despair. But Casilda had heard about a miraculous spring in a Christian country and she just knew she would be healed if she went there. So, because her father loved her very much, he let her go.

And she was healed! But after that she had a decision to make. She couldn't be a Christian if she went home, but she couldn't live without Jesus. Without a second thought, Casilda chose Jesus and sent her attendants home without her. The princess lived the rest of her life a hermit in the forest—until she was one hundred years old! With no family and no fancy clothes and no palace, St. Casilda of Toledo was finally happy.

St. Casilda is standing in a typical Moorish archway. Bold jewelry and bright colors were popular in Moorish fashion, as were beautiful patterns like the intricate embroidery on Casilda's dress. Women often wore loose-fitting pants, as Casilda is under her dress. In this picture Casilda has chosen (like many royal women) not to cover her head. She is placing bread in a basket to bring to her friends in prison.

Bl. Cecilia Butsi Wongwai

Cecilia BOOHT-see WONG-why
(BOOHT like book but with a t)
Thailand | 1924–1940
Feast Day: December 26

Have you ever heard the story of a martyr who went singing to her death and wondered if maybe the storyteller was exaggerating a little bit? You can be willing to die for Jesus, sure, but it's hard to imagine being really happy about it.

Bl. Cecilia Butsi Wongwai was.

People who watched her die were asked about it, and this is what they said:

She skipped.

Cecilia was sixteen years old when the police made the village's priest leave the country and killed Bl. Philip Siphon Onphitak, the village catechist. After that, the police stood outside the Catholic school shooting their guns in the air and shouting at the Sisters to stop teaching the faith.

But Cecilia, who worked for the Sisters, wasn't frightened. She knew that people who gave their lives for Jesus found themselves in his arms. So when the police chief called a meeting to tell the Catholics of Songkhon to abandon their faith, Cecilia stood up and began to shout that she would never deny Jesus. The police ignored her. Her friends and family shushed her. They were scared—but not Cecilia.

The Sisters weren't afraid, either. On Christmas Day, the police chief told the Sisters he would kill them if they didn't stop talking about Jesus.

"Do you really mean you will kill us for being Christians?" Sr. Agnes asked.

"I do!" he growled.

Sr. Agnes looked him right in the eye and said, "Be sure you bring enough bullets."

How terribly brave of her! And when he left, Sr. Agnes (who later became Bl. Agnes Phila) didn't pack her things and sneak away. Instead, she wrote a letter saying that the Christians of Songkhon would never deny Jesus, no matter what happened to them. Then Cecilia took that letter to the police, skipping as she went. On her way back, she said goodbye to some friends. "I'm on my way to heaven!" she called.

Some martyrs are terrified. They grit their teeth and set their faces and go trembling to their deaths. It's not a sin to be scared. But Cecilia was excited. The next day, when the police came for them, Bl. Cecilia Butsi Wongwai and the other martyrs went singing to their deaths. They really and truly did.

Bl. Cecilia Butsi is dancing for joy on her way to be martyred. She's dressed in the traditional garb of Thai peasants, made of fabric called mo hom, and the positions of her hands and feet remind us of beautiful Thai dances. The clouds are drawn in the style of many Thai artists.

Bl. Ceferino Giménez Malla

sef-er-EE-no hee-MEN-ess MY-ah
Spain | 1861–1936
Feast Day: August 2

Nobody expected the roving horse trader to become an old man who went to daily Mass. And nobody expected the sweet, winking grandpa to become a martyr. But Bl. Ceferino Giménez Malla wasn't what anybody expected.

Ceferino was born into a family of wandering basket weavers. They were Roma (a kind of people often called "Gypsies") and even though they lived in Spain, they were very different from the Spaniards. People are sometimes cruel when somebody is different, and a lot of people were unkind to the Roma, calling them liars and thieves. Ceferino could have decided to hate everyone who treated his people badly. Or he could have decided to turn his back on his people. But Ceferino didn't see why he had to choose. So he decided to love everybody.

When he grew up, Ceferino became a horse trader. He was good with horses and he was a good businessman, though he never learned to read or write. But mostly he was good at loving his wife, his adopted daughter, and eventually his grandchildren. He loved dancing and village fairs. He loved giving little children chocolates and telling them stories about Jesus, and they loved listening.

Ceferino was kind and gentle and funny. He was a really good friend and soon became holy, too, but not in a showy way.

He didn't work miracles or see visions—he just went to Mass every day, prayed the Rosary, and helped the poor. He worked hard and made lots of money, but he gave it all away. He was just an ordinary old man who loved Jesus and Mary.

But Ceferino lived in a dangerous time, and one day he saw soldiers hurting a priest. He ran over to stop them, and when they asked if he had a weapon, he pulled out his rosary and said, "Only this."

Well you can bet the soldiers didn't like that! They arrested the old man and threw him in jail. When he got there, he just kept praying the Rosary. A friend begged him to stop praying so loudly, but Ceferino wouldn't abandon God. And so Bl. Ceferino Giménez Malla was killed for the faith that had given him so much, an ordinary old Roma man who had secretly been a hero all along.

Bl. Ceferino is leading one of his beautiful horses, with his daughter Pepita sitting astride the horse. He's wearing one of his fine suits and carrying the rosary for which he gave his life. Hanging at his side are his stable keys, which were found after his death and are revered as a relic along with his rosary.

Bl. Ceferino Namuncurá

sef-er-EE-no nah-MOOHN-coo-RA
Argentina, Italy | 1886–1905
Feast Day: August 26

P eople thought Bl. Ceferino Namuncurá couldn't really be a Mapuche if he was Catholic, and they thought he couldn't really be Catholic if he was Mapuche. His father was the chief of the Mapuches, a tribe of Native Argentineans who had been at war for many years, first with Spanish colonizers and then with the Argentinean army. Just before Ceferino's birth, his people had surrendered. They hoped to continue their way of life but knew they had to work with the people who had invaded their land. So when he was eleven, Ceferino was sent to a Spanish-speaking school to learn to lead his people by walking in both worlds.

But Ceferino was the only Indigenous child in the school and the other students were sometimes cruel. Even when he transferred to a Catholic school, he found that the boys believed some very racist things. When another boy asked Ceferino what human flesh tasted like, poor Ceferino just began to cry quietly. How could these boys who he thought were his friends believe that Ceferino and his family were cannibals?

It hurt Ceferino dreadfully, but he was a gentle soul who wanted to make friends. So he showed the other boys card tricks, went hunting with them, sang in the choir, and taught them how to shoot a bow and arrow. And he received Communion as often as he could, spoke kindly, and offered his suffering to the Lord. In a quiet way, he was becoming a Saint.

All the time that he was in school, Ceferino dreamed of bringing his people to Jesus. He knew that as a priest, he would be able to go to his people and teach them that God loved them just as much as he loved the people who had conquered them. So Ceferino entered the Salesian order to study for the priesthood. But he had become very ill, and though he was taken to Italy to seek a cure, Ceferino died when he was only eighteen. In life, Bl. Ceferino Namuncurá had no chance to bring his people to Jesus, but since his death, his prayers and his example have brought thousands and thousands of Mapuches to know the Lord, fully Catholic and fully Mapuche.

Bl. Ceferino's people are famous for their skill as weavers; here, he's dressed in a traditional Mapuche makuñ (poncho). Behind him is a Criollo horse, the type of horse he grew up riding and on which he learned to be an excellent horseman. Each year, many devotees ride on a horseback pilgrimage to Ceferino's birthplace to celebrate his feast day.

Bl. Columba Kang Wan-suk

col-UM-ba KAHNG wahn-SOOK
South Korea | 1761–1801
Feast Day: July 2

Bl. Columba Kang Wan-suk wasn't supposed to be in charge. Everyone expected her to be gentle and quiet because she was a woman. But Columba was strong and brave and brilliant and she didn't listen to what everyone expected of her. If she had, the whole history of Korea might have been different.

Columba was a noblewoman, wife, mother, and stepmother. More importantly, she was a brand new Christian in a country where the Gospel had only been discovered about fifteen years earlier. As soon as she heard about Jesus, she wanted to tell everyone! Her mother-in-law listened. So did her stepson, Bl. Philip Hong Pil-ju. But her husband did not. He didn't like Columba much, and he especially didn't like her telling him what to do. So he told her to move out and not come back.

A divorce is a really hard thing, even if your husband wasn't very kind, but Columba trusted that God was going to use this hard thing to do something wonderful. And soon she realized that now that she had her own home, the government wouldn't search it. She could hide people in her house to protect them! So she gathered lots of Christian ladies, especially the ones who had made vows of virginity. And pretty soon, she was hiding

a priest—the first priest ever to serve in Korea! For six years, clever Columba kept Bl. James Zhou Wen-mo safe, smuggling him from one house to the next so he could hear Confessions and celebrate Mass for the thousands of Korean Catholics who had never seen a priest before.

But her job wasn't just to take care of the priest. No, Fr. Zhou had made Columba a catechist, a person who teaches about Jesus. Because she was so wise and brave and strong, Columba brought dozens of people to Jesus—even two princesses—all while keeping the whole Church in Korea safe and running. Eventually, she was arrested for her faith. When her captors found out what a leader Columba was in the Church, they were shocked. How could a woman do such things? But Bl. Columba Kang Wan-suk had never much worried about what people would think. She only cared about what God thought, which is what made her a Christian, a leader, a martyr, and an example for the whole Church.

Bl. Columba is standing (as she so often did) as protector of the persecuted Christian community. She's shown with one of the many women she evangelized and catechized: her mother-in-law, who broke with tradition by leaving her own son behind so that she could continue living with Columba after Columba's divorce. Beside her are Bl. James Zhou Wen-mo (the Chinese priest Columba protected in Korea for six years) and Columba's stepson, Bl. Philip Hong Pil-ju.

St. Columba of Iona

col-UM-ba of eye-OH-na
Ireland, Scotland | 521–597
Feast Day: June 9

St. Columba of Iona should have known better.

Sometimes we hear about Saints who did wicked things before they knew God, so we think, "I guess they didn't know any better."

But Columba had practically been born a monk. He'd gone to live with monks when he was only a little boy and he joined them when he was barely a grown-up. Then he became a priest and traveled around Ireland to preach and found monasteries. Everybody must have thought he was awfully holy!

But when things didn't go Columba's way, look out.

Finnian, another monk (and later Saint), had gotten a copy of the Psalms, translated by St. Jerome. Columba thought it was a wonderful book and asked Finnian if he could copy it. But Finnian (who also should have known better) was very proud that his was the only copy in Ireland, and he said no.

That wasn't fair. Finnian shouldn't have been so selfish, especially not with the Word of God. So Columba started copying the book in secret. Finnian found out and demanded the copy Columba had made.

Well, he wasn't about to hand it over! So he yelled and fought and finally demanded that the king tell him he was right. But the king took Finnian's side and told that thief Columba he couldn't keep the book.

Columba was SO MAD. So he started a war. And got three thousand people killed.

I told you he should have known better! After the war was over, Columba realized what he had done. He felt terrible, but it was too late. He couldn't bring all those men back.

Do you think God still loved him? Absolutely he did! God loves everybody, always, no matter what. Still, the bishops of Ireland told Columba that he had to go away from his country and never come back.

Columba was heartbroken, but God is very good, and he took Columba's big, bad mistake and used it to do something wonderful. Columba sailed to Scotland to teach people about Jesus. Before long, all of Scotland was Christian! All because St. Columba of Iona had done a wicked thing when he should have known better and our amazing God had turned it to good.

St. Columba is standing in the rolling hills of Ireland, preparing for his exile to Scotland. He often said that the breezes on the fair hills of Ireland were like the gentle winds of paradise to him, and he lamented how he would miss them. The dove symbolizes not only the Holy Spirit but also Columba's name, which means dove in both Irish ("Colm") and Latin ("Columba").

Bl. Concepción Cabrera de Armida

cone-sep-SYONE cah-BREH-ra deh
ar-MEE-da | Conchita: cone-CHEE-ta
Mexico | 1862–1937
Feast Day: March 3

What would you do if you found out that your mom was going to be made a Saint? That in all the years of reading you stories and taking you places she was also having visions and writing sixty thousand pages of things Jesus had told her?

That's what happened to Bl. Concepción Cabrera de Armida's children. They had always known their mom was holy, but they had no idea how holy.

Some people may have been surprised that Concepción (who was always called Conchita) didn't want to be a nun. Often people think that holy people have to be priests and nuns. But really you can be holy in any state of life, and Conchita knew God was calling her to marriage.

When she was thirteen, Conchita was at a dance and fell in love with a boy named Pancho. Nine years later, when they married, Conchita asked him for a gift: would he help her go to Mass every day? Pancho said yes, and for the rest of their married life he made sure Conchita was at Mass every day, often sending her out the door as he watched the children.

And they had a lot of children—nine all together. Conchita was *very* busy cooking and cleaning and raising her children. Still, there was always time for Jesus because Conchita made time.

When poor Conchita was only thirty-nine, and her children were all still young, Pancho died. She was heartbroken, but as much as she had loved her husband, she always loved Jesus more. So she accepted her cross and kept going. Because while Conchita was so busy with her family, she was also hearing the voice of Jesus and seeing him in prayer. For nearly forty years as a widow, Conchita brought people to Jesus. She started an order of Sisters and groups for lay people and even an order of priests (which is an amazing thing for a woman to do) all while loving her children and grandchildren well.

Bl. Concepción Cabrera de Armida was a wife, a mother, and a grandmother—and a mystic, a writer, and a leader in the Church. It turns out that if you give your life to Jesus you can do some pretty amazing things, even if the people around you don't always notice.

Bl. Concepción is shown with her husband and all nine of her children. Pancho is beside her with a mustache. The religious Sister is her daughter Concepción, who joined the Sisters of the Cross of the Sacred Heart of Jesus (founded by Conchita), and the priest is her son Manuel, who became a Jesuit. Pablo (eighteen years old), Carlos (six years old), and Pedrito (three years old) all died young and are shown in faded colors to indicate their death.

Bl. Cyprian Michael Iwene Tansi

SIP-ree-uhn Michael ee-WEH-neh
TAHN-see
Nigeria, England | 1903–1964
Feast Day: January 20

Bl. Cyprian Michael Iwene Tansi's life sure looked like a waste. He had become Catholic when he was nine, and when he told his family that God was calling him to be a priest, they were not pleased. Why would he not get married? Why would he not work to provide for his family? What a waste.

But Fr. Cyprian became a really good priest. He helped his people build houses, rode his bike from one village to another, heard Confessions for hours and hours, and brought lots of people to Jesus. He defended the rights of women, who were often treated very badly. Once, he was riding his bicycle when he saw a woman being attacked by a group of men. Fr. Cyprian jumped off his bike and ran to fight them off with her. Then he helped her to be brave and take those wicked men to court. He loved her like a dad, which is just the way he loved all his people.

Fr. Cyprian didn't live in a fine home like most of the priests in Nigeria did. He didn't even ask his people to buy him a car; instead, he used his bike to go all around his huge parishes. He was such a good witness that seventy men from his parishes went on to become priests.

Fr. Cyprian was doing good work for the Lord, but he felt a tug on his heart. God was asking him to give up his ministry and become a monk. So he made the long journey to England, where he didn't get to do any of the amazing work he had done before. His job was just to learn. For years he wasn't even allowed to hear Confessions. What a waste!

But Fr. Cyprian was spending his days in prayer, and time in prayer is never wasted. Neither is a life handed over to God. And even though Fr. Cyprian never got to go back to Africa and never did any obviously useful work again, his prayers did more good than all his years of ministry. "If you are going to be a Christian at all, you might as well live entirely for God," Bl. Cyprian Michael Iwene Tansi said, and that's what he did. Even when it looked like a waste.

Bl. Cyprian is wearing a white cassock, common in warmer climates where the hot sun makes wearing black imprudent. Behind him are the homes he helped his people build, using new techniques that he taught them and bricks he made himself. Propped against a nearby hut is a Hercules bicycle, a brand popular in Nigeria at the time; he may have ridden one just like it from one village to another to serve his people.

St. Damien of Molokai

DAY-mee-uhn of MOLE-oh-kie
(more accurately, MOLE-oh-kah-EE)
Belgium, United States | 1840–1889
Feast Day: May 10

 Damien of Molokai was an awfully hard worker. But when he tried to become a priest, his superiors didn't care how hard he worked. They told him he wasn't smart enough to be a priest. How do you think that made him feel? I bet it really hurt his feelings. But Damien knew that God was calling him to be a priest, so he trusted that God would make up for all the parts of him that other people said weren't good enough.

Pretty soon, his order needed priests to go on the long journey to Hawaii. Br. Damien made one argument after another until he convinced his superiors that they should send him. And it's a good thing they did! After he was ordained, he found out that his parish was huge and full of mountains. He didn't need to be very smart to get around; he needed to be a hard worker.

Hard work was even more important when Fr. Damien went to Molokai, the island where people were sent when they got the terrible, painful disease of leprosy. Fr. Damien knew how much Jesus had loved the lepers, so he asked to go serve the lepers of Molokai. Even though it meant that he might never be able to leave. Even though he might get leprosy. He loved his people, so he went.

But when he got there, Fr. Damien found that many of the people were too sad and lonely and angry to want to hear about Jesus. He couldn't win them over with clever homilies, so he dug graves and built coffins and cleaned their wounds instead. Then he helped them start a choir and a band and even organized footraces between them. He worked hard to show them God's love, and soon they wanted to be Christians. Fr. Damien's love and witness had given them hope.

Fr. Damien didn't try to protect himself from the disease his people had. He came right into their lives and loved them, even though he knew it might hurt him. And in the end, it did. St. Damien of Molokai died of leprosy, but he wasn't sorry for a minute. He had worked hard to love his people well, and his love had helped them come to know Jesus.

St. Damien is standing in front of the Church of St. Philomena on Molokai; though a very small chapel was there when he arrived, Fr. Damien expanded it to the beautiful stone structure still standing today. Not visible behind him is the graveyard where he buried his people and where he was buried himself. The lei around his neck symbolizes the welcome he ultimately received from the patients on Molokai.

Bl. Daudi Okelo & Bl. Jildo Irwa

DOW-dee oh-KEH-lo and
JEEL-do EER-wa
Uganda | 1902–1918, 1906–1918
Feast Day: September 18

Bl. Daudi Okelo and Bl. Jildo Irwa were a great team. Daudi was shy and quiet, while Jildo was loud and outgoing. Both boys were raised in non-Christian families and both decided on their own to become Christian. They studied the faith for two years before finally being baptized.

Less than a year later, Daudi heard that his cousin Antonio, a catechist in the village of Paimol, had died of influenza. Daudi was heartbroken, but he had an idea: what if he went to replace Antonio? And what if he took Jildo with him?

Daudi was only fifteen years old and Jildo just eleven. And this wasn't a trip across town to teach Sunday school. The boys would have to travel almost fifty miles through a land where wicked men were kidnapping people to sell them into slavery. When they got to Paimol, they would face famine and influenza, not to mention the many people who hated Christianity. The priest in charge told Daudi and Jildo how dangerous it would all be.

"And you, Jildo, are so small!" he warned.

"But Daudi is big," Jildo replied.

"I do not fear death." Daudi said. "Did not Jesus also die for us?"

Well, nobody could argue against courage like that. It took months, but eventually the boys were sent to Paimol. There, Daudi would beat a drum every morning to call people together for catechism class. Then he would teach large groups (even though he was shy and a little nervous). Jildo, on the other hand, led the children in loud, wild games. He was so much fun that everyone loved him. And because they loved Jildo, they listened to Daudi.

After morning catechism, the two boys worked in the field all day and taught more lessons in the evening. For nearly a year, they preached the Word of God to many eager listeners in the village.

But Daudi and Jildo had enemies, men who hated Christianity and would do anything to stop it from spreading. They brought weapons to threaten the boys with, telling them they should leave Paimol and not come back. But the holy catechists could not be silent with such good news to share, and they said so. A team to the end, Bl. Daudi Okelo and Bl. Jildo Irwa were killed for their faith.

At the shrine of Bls. Daudi and Jildo, there are two arches built embracing each other to symbolize the boys' friendship. Daudi and Jildo are standing under these arches, wearing their white catechist's robes and the medals of Our Lady that they received when they became catechumens. Their books (the catechism of St. Pius X translated into Acholi) symbolize that they were catechists and the colors of the image call to mind the Ugandan flag.

Bl. Denis of the Nativity

France, Indonesia | 1600–1638
Feast Day: November 29

Bl. Denis of the Nativity wanted an adventure.

The son of a French navy captain, Denis had gone to sea when he was only twelve years old, a little scrap of a sailor. By nineteen, he had made his way to Asia and was soon piloting ships around the tiny islands of Indonesia.

Denis wasn't just a good sailor. He was excellent at languages and had a brilliant mind for maps, reading them and drawing them. Before he was thirty, Denis was in charge of a fleet of ships sent to save the city of Malacca from a besieging enemy. When Denis and his navy won the day, he was hailed as a hero, knighted, and made pilot-in-chief as well as cosmographer (which means astronomer and geographer) to the king of Portugal. What an adventure!

But guns and ships and foreign lands weren't enough for Sir Denis. His heart longed for more. And while he was all set to have an amazing career at sea, with money and power and fame for the taking, Sir Denis knew that would never make him happy.

So the sea captain traded in his uniform for a habit, leaving behind the freedom of the high seas for a friar's cell. Sir Denis became a Carmelite priest. And though he may have thought fondly of his days at sea, he knew that part of his life was over.

Until it wasn't. The Portuguese ambassador was signing a treaty with the King of Achem (in what's now Indonesia) and he needed Fr. Denis. He needed his skill as a sailor and a linguist and a strategist. But he also needed a priest, a spiritual counselor. So Fr. Denis went on one last voyage.

They were met at the port of Achem with honors, but the whole thing was a trap. The men were taken to prison, where their captors insisted that they deny Jesus and convert to Islam. Fr. Denis had been brave in battle and he was brave in martyrdom. He and his friends refused to deny the God who loved them, and each was killed in turn. And so Bl. Denis of the Nativity, who had given up adventuring to be faithful to God's call, had his greatest adventure yet and won a martyr's crown.

Bl. Denis was described by his friends as blond and adventurous. Here he's wearing his Carmelite habit and sailing in a ship modeled on Ferdinand Magellan's Portuguese fleet. He has his rosary in one hand and his map and spyglass in the other, ready to help the captain pilot his ship and to offer prayers, too.

Bl. Dina Bélanger

DEE-nah BAY-lon-ZHAY
Canada | 1897–1929
Feast Day: September 4

If you loved playing piano and were so good at it that you had studied at a conservatory in New York City and were playing concerts in Quebec City, what could make you quit? If you composed beautiful music and were surrounded by people who admired you, what could make you give it all up? Only love.

That's what Bl. Dina Bélanger discovered. And it wasn't just that she was willing to give it up for love of Jesus—she loved Jesus so much, she didn't really want anything but him.

Dina was an only child and her parents loved her so much that it would have been very easy for her to be spoiled. It was in her nature to be stubborn and defiant, and once she decided to do something, nothing could stop her. But as a very little girl Dina decided that the one thing she wanted, the thing she would get no matter what, was holiness. So she took all her stubbornness and determination and fixed it on heaven.

You may think that since Dina was stubborn she must have been loud and outgoing. But really she was very shy. She didn't like noisy games or lots of attention, and while she enjoyed spending time with a friend or two, Dina was quite happy being alone.

That may be part of why it was so easy for Dina to leave behind the amazing life she was leading. It wasn't really what she wanted, after all. She wanted to be still with Jesus. But the real reason Dina gave up her life as a performer was that she had been hearing the voice of Jesus for years, and now he was telling her to come follow him. So Dina became a Sister.

Though she really wanted to be a cloistered nun, Dina knew that God was asking her to use her gift of music as a teacher. So she entered a teaching community, where her visions continued and her writing became more and more beautiful. But the good Sister had tuberculosis (which meant she was often too sick to teach) and died of her disease after only eight years in the convent. Bl. Dina Bélanger had given up everything the world had to offer and died at only thirty-two. She had no regrets.

Bl. Dina has just finished a piano performance in Quebec City. She's holding a beautiful (and complex) piece she composed called "Ricordanza," which you can listen to online. When Dina entered religious life, she took the name Marie of Ste-Cécile de Rome after St. Cecilia of Rome, the famous patron Saint of music.

St. Dulce Pontes

DOOL-see POHN-cheess
Brazil | 1914–1992
Feast Day: August 13

You would think that a woman who broke the window of a crashed bus to pull a dozen people to safety before the bus burst into flames must be some sort of superhero, right? Well, I suppose she was—a superhero Sister who used her powers to help save the poor.

St. Dulce Pontes didn't set out to be a hero. She just wanted to help suffering people. So when she was young, she told the poor they could come to her house if they needed a snack or a haircut or some medicine. Even when she became a Sister she didn't have big plans to change the world. No, Sr. Dulce just wanted to do small things with great love. So she fed one child. Found a home for one family. Taught one man to read.

Pretty soon, all Sr. Dulce's small things began to add up to some really big things. She started a school for the poor, an orphanage, and a nursing home. And she found homes for a lot of different people. The trouble was, the homes Sr. Dulce found weren't exactly hers to give away, and her friends kept getting kicked out. Sr. Dulce moved them from one abandoned building to another until she finally brought them all home to her convent. They lived in the chicken yard at first, but over time Sr. Dulce built up a whole hospital that's still there today.

Sr. Dulce wasn't very strong. She had a really hard time breathing. But she didn't let that stop her. If she found a man on the street who was too weak to walk, Sr. Dulce would pick him up and carry him to her hospital. If she found children who were sad and lonely, she would play soccer with them or play her accordion. And when she saw that bus crash, she didn't stop to think about herself. She just ran outside, broke the window, and started dragging people out. Sr. Dulce had become a hero without even noticing!

By the end of her life, everyone knew how wonderful Sr. Dulce was. Pope St. John Paul II came to visit her. So did the president of Brazil. She was even nominated for a Nobel Prize! And all because the little things she did built her up into a hero and a Saint.

St. Dulce is wearing the habit of the Missionaries of the Immaculate Conception. She's visiting her young friends in a favela, a Brazilian shanty town that was built out of whatever discarded materials were available, even old tires. She brought her accordion to play for the people she was visiting and her soccer ball to play with them. The chickens remind us of the chicken yard that Sr. Dulce once turned into a hospital for the poor.

St. Elizabeth Hesselblad

Elizabeth HESS-uhl-BLAHD
Sweden, Italy | 1870–1957
Feast Day: April 24

St. Elizabeth Hesselblad didn't want to be wrong. And when she realized that there were divisions in the Church, she wasn't sure which one was right. Growing up in Sweden, she belonged to the Lutheran Church, a Christian community that disagrees with the Catholic Church on some pretty important things. But when she moved to New York City and studied to be a nurse, she met Catholics for the first time and began to wonder if this wasn't the one flock of Jesus.

Then one day, Elizabeth found herself in a crowd as a Eucharistic procession passed by. When everybody else knelt before Jesus in the Blessed Sacrament, Elizabeth backed away. She didn't want to kneel to a piece of bread—that would be really wrong. But suddenly, she heard Jesus say, "I am he whom you seek." Elizabeth fell to her knees, certain that the host was truly God.

After that, Elizabeth began to read everything she could find about the Catholic Church. Once she knew what was right, nothing could stop her from becoming Catholic. She went straight to a priest she'd never met before and asked to become Catholic immediately. After asking her a lot of questions, he agreed to baptize her only three days later!

Elizabeth was overjoyed to be a Catholic, but it broke her heart to be separated from her Lutheran family and from the rest of the Swedish people, almost none of whom are Catholic. So she asked God what he wanted from her, and pretty soon she had an answer: she needed to work to end the divisions among Christians by loving everybody, no matter what. So Elizabeth refounded the Bridgettine order, originally founded by St. Bridget of Sweden (one of the last Swedish Saints before Elizabeth herself).

Sr. Elizabeth opened a convent in Sweden, then in England and Switzerland and even India. And when World War II threatened Jews throughout Europe, Sr. Elizabeth's love of non-Catholics led her to hide twelve Jewish people in her convent in Rome to save them from certain death. She helped Jews and Protestants and communists, who believed in no God. At home in the Catholic Church, St. Elizabeth Hesselblad didn't worry about being wrong anymore, which left her so much more time to love.

St. Elizabeth is wearing the habit of the Bridgettine order that she refounded. A crown is worn over the veil; its five red spots signify the five wounds of Christ, while the grey of the habit represents sacrifices made in reparation for sins. Sr. Elizabeth is standing at the edge of Runn Lake in Falun, Sweden, the town where she spent her childhood. After her death, her order established a house with this view of the lake.

Bl. Emilian Kovch

em-EEL-yan KOHFCH
Ukraine, Poland | 1884–1944
Feast Day: March 25

 Emilian Kovch never abandoned anyone, no matter what it cost him.

Emilian belonged to the Ukrainian Greek Catholic Church, a Catholic Church that believes everything the pope believes but has some different rules from the Roman Catholic Church. One big difference is that married men can become priests, so Emilian got married and became a priest.

But Fr. Emilian lived in a very dangerous time, and while he was taking care of the poor and organizing pilgrimages, he was also fighting prejudice. He told Ukrainians not to hate Poles and then when the Nazis came and told everybody that they should hate the Jewish people, Fr. Emilian preached against anti-Semitism (hatred for Jews), too.

Fr. Emilian even baptized Jewish people to try to protect them from the Nazis. And one time, when Nazi soldiers had driven lots of Jews into a synagogue and were throwing firebombs at it to burn it down, Fr. Emilian came running through the streets to stop them. He planted his feet on the steps of the synagogue and shouted at those soldiers until they felt ashamed and went away. Then Fr. Emilian ran into the burning building to bring people out to safety.

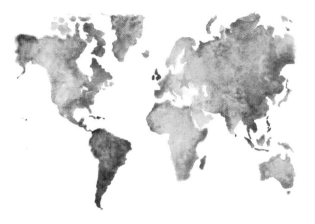

Fr. Emilian was a hero! But the Nazis sure didn't think so. They didn't like how he cared for the weak and the outcast. They didn't like that he wasn't afraid of them. So they arrested him and sent him off to a concentration camp, an extra-bad prison where they took people (mostly innocent people) to kill them.

I don't have to tell you that Fr. Emilian's family was heartbroken. His children began to write letter after letter trying to win their father's freedom. But then they got a letter from their dad. "I understand that you are trying to get me released. But I beg you not to do this. If I am not here, who will help them to get through these sufferings?" Fr. Emilian was the only priest in that concentration camp, and he knew he needed to stay to hear the prisoners' Confessions and give them Communion. And so, even though it meant leaving his wife and children behind, even though he knew it might kill him, Bl. Emilian Kovch stayed. He stayed and he served and he died for love of Jesus and his people.

Bl. Emilian is shown both before and after his interment in Majdanek concentration camp. On the left, he's wearing Byzantine vestments and standing before the burning synagogue of Przemysl. On the right, he's wearing a prison uniform, with a red triangle to show that he was a political prisoner. He's holding his hand up in a sign of the Trinity, because he refused to stop baptizing in the name of the Trinity even to save his life.

St. Ephrem the Syrian

EFF-rem the SEER-ee-an
Syria, Turkey | 306–373
Feast Day: June 9

What would you do if everybody around you believed lies about Jesus? If some people believed that Jesus wasn't really God and some people believed the Holy Spirit wasn't God and some people thought our bodies were evil? Would you write books to tell them the truth? Or preach homilies explaining what's right?

St. Ephrem the Syrian preached and wrote books, but if you want souls to be saved, sometimes you have to be creative. So Ephrem began to write songs. He knew that it's easy to ignore preachers and writers, but music is different. Music gets stuck in your head. It stays with you, so you can't forget as easily. And music is a way of worshiping. Ephrem knew that if he could teach people to sing about who God is, he could get them to love God—the true God: Father, Son, and Holy Spirit.

So Ephrem began to write. He wrote hundreds and hundreds of hymns and taught them to women's choirs so that they would spread to everyone. Ephrem was a deacon, so he wrote homilies, too (though even then he sometimes preached in poetry). And he wrote books.

But it wasn't enough for Ephrem to talk about Jesus, he had to live what he taught.

When war drove the Christians out of his hometown, Ephrem went into exile with them. And when a famine in the land left them starving, he went to the rich who were hoarding food and demanded that they share. Only Ephrem was trusted to be honest and fair in distributing food, so he was in charge of feeding everyone who was hungry. Later, when a plague hit the city, Ephrem left the cave where he lived to take care of the sick and dying until he caught the plague himself and died.

After his death, people talked about how kind Ephrem had been, and how generous. But seventeen hundred years later, what we remember most about St. Ephrem the Syrian is his music and his poetry. We remember the way his love of God poured out in song, in hymns that taught the faithful and led them to worship. And some people still sing those hymns, grateful for a teacher who was willing to be creative.

St. Ephrem's name means fruitful. As a child, he had a vision that a grapevine sprang from his tongue and bore fruit; this vine surrounds him here. His right hand is making the symbol of the Trinity. The Syriac on his scroll says, "Blessed is he whose workers remain in his vineyard." The upper left corner shows Ephrem's nickname, the Harp of the Spirit; Mary is in the upper right because of Ephrem's many Marian hymns.

St. Eulalia of Mérida

you-LAY-lee-ah of MARE-ih-da
Spain | 292–304
Feast Day: December 10

St. Eulalia of Mérida was gentle and sweet and pleasant.

Except when she wasn't. Because while it's good to be gentle and sweet and pleasant most of the time, sometimes you have to be strong and stern and forceful instead.

Though she was only twelve, Eulalia had been consecrated as a bride of Jesus. And when her parents discovered that Christians were being martyred in their town, they knew Eulalia was in trouble—not because she might be caught but because they were sure that as soon as she found out she would march right into the court and shout at the government officials who were doing such wicked things. And while they were proud of their daughter's faith, they didn't want her killed.

So Eulalia's parents took her to the country, hoping she wouldn't find out about the persecutions. But she did. And once Eulalia realized what was happening, she knew she had to do something about it. She climbed out of her window (which was a very naughty and dangerous thing to do) and snuck back to Mérida.

Once she was there, Eulalia stormed furiously up to the wicked judge and began to yell. Normally the judge would have had someone killed on the spot for talking to him that way, but Eulalia was so little and so cute! So he spoke to her like she was throwing a silly tantrum, telling her just to worship the idol a little bit.

How do you think Eulalia felt about that? Well, how do you feel when you're very upset about something and grown-ups act like you're just being a silly child? Eulalia was fuming—not just for her sake, but for God's sake. And suddenly, she wasn't a bit sweet and gentle. No, she was spitting mad. And so she did a dreadfully rude thing that you must never, ever do (unless a pagan judge is trying to force you to worship a false god).

She spat in the judge's face.

Then she kicked over his false gods. Well that judge was just as angry as you would imagine—so angry that he had Eulalia martyred. St. Eulalia of Mérida had known how to control her temper and she had known when to let it fly. And God used all of her for his glory.

St. Eulalia is at the Roman Forum in Mérida, standing between the interior columns of what's called the Temple of Diana (though later research has revealed that this temple was devoted to the imperial cult). She is trampling an idol of Diana, the virgin goddess of wisdom whose purity and wisdom were dwarfed by Eulalia's.

St. Faustina Kowalska

faw-STEE-nah ko-VAL-ska
Poland | 1905–1938
Feast Day: October 5

It isn't always easy to do God's will. For St. Faustina Kowalska, it meant being ignored and laughed at. It meant being weak and sick. But it also meant changing the world.

Faustina felt called to be a Sister, but her parents told her no. So she decided to buy beautiful clothes, go out dancing, and enjoy herself. She wasn't sinning, exactly, but she wasn't following God's call. Then one night, Faustina was at a party when she saw Jesus standing before her, bloody and suffering. "How long will you make me wait?" he asked.

So she left. She didn't pack a bag. She didn't say goodbye to her parents. She went straight to Warsaw to enter the convent—but none of the convents wanted her! Poor Faustina tried one community after another. Finally somebody said she could stay, so Sr. Faustina settled into being an ordinary Sister. She wasn't a particularly good worker, and she was often sick (which annoyed the other Sisters, who rolled their eyes and put up with her). But all the while, Sr. Faustina was having incredible visions. Jesus appeared to her again and again, asking her to tell the world about his mercy. At first, Sr. Faustina tried to ignore him; she wasn't used to being unusual and she was pretty scared. But finally she realized that she couldn't avoid Jesus if she loved him, so she started to listen.

Jesus wanted Sr. Faustina to teach the world to say, "Jesus, I trust in you." He kept appearing to Sr. Faustina, which was a great gift to her. But life was still hard. She was sick all the time. Some of the priests and Sisters she told about her visions thought that she was crazy or that she was lying. And sometimes it was so, so difficult to feel God's love.

But Sr. Faustina didn't give up on Jesus. She didn't ignore her visions or leave her convent. She didn't try to make her life easy, because she trusted that God was working in all the hard things in her life. And today, the world is different because of her faithfulness. Through St. Faustina Kowalska, God told everyone of his great mercy, and all because she did his will even when it was hard.

St. Faustina is wearing the habit of the Sisters of Our Lady of Mercy and holding the image of Divine Mercy that Jesus told her to have painted. He is appearing to her as he is shown in the image, his right hand blessing and his left pointing toward his heart from which pour out red rays (symbolizing his Blood) and white rays (symbolizing the water that poured from the side of Christ and the waters of baptism).

Bl. Francisca de Paula de Jesus

fruhn-SEES-kah jih POW-lah jih zheh-ZOOS | Nhá Chica: nyah SHEE-kah
Brazil | 1810–1895
Feast Day: June 14

Everybody should have looked down on Bl. Francisca de Paula de Jesus. She had been enslaved. She couldn't read. She was an orphan. She was poor. Most people would say she had nothing at all to offer.

Maybe they did say that. But Nhá Chica (which means "Aunt Francie") never cared what anyone thought. She just did what she knew she needed to do, and everybody else could take it or leave it.

Nhá Chica had been born into slavery, with only a mother and a brother to love her. They were freed when Nhá Chica was ten, but soon after that her mother died, leaving behind nothing but a statue of the Immaculate Conception. Nhá Chica must have been awfully sad to lose her mother, but she was also very determined: she wasn't going to belong to anybody but Jesus ever again. She wasn't going to marry anybody. She wasn't even going to live with her brother. From now on, it would be Nhá Chica and Jesus alone, with Mary as her mother.

Nhá Chica spent her days begging, but even though she was terribly poor, she didn't keep the food she was given. No, she and her brother begged for other people. They became some of the most generous philanthropists around even though they didn't have a penny to their names.

That was how people first started to learn how holy Nhá Chica was. But as the years went on, they began to see that she was also really wise. This penniless, illiterate woman gave such good advice that even businessmen and politicians came to ask for her insight. She organized prayer meetings and hosted a weekly lunch for the hungry, and when her brother died and left her an inheritance, she used most of it to build a Marian chapel to hold her statue of Mary and gave the rest to the poor.

The world might have seen Nhá Chica as worthless, but she never once listened to what the world said. She heard only the love of God. And by listening to his voice she lived a life that left people lining up for a word of wisdom from an uneducated, illiterate, former slave—a brilliant and beloved child of God, that is. Because that's what Bl. Francisca de Paula de Jesus truly was.

Nhá Chica is standing in front of the Church of the Immaculate Conception, which was built on the site of her Chapel of the Immaculate Conception. Above the door of the new church is a statue of Christ the Redeemer, just like the one in Rio de Janeiro, Brazil. Nhá Chica's hands are cupped before her, either begging for money or giving some away.

St. Germaine Cousin

juhr-MAIN coo-ZAN
France | 1579–1601
Feast Day: June 15

St. Germaine Cousin was a real-life Cinderella: a sweet, hard-working girl with a wicked stepmother. Now, most stepmothers are good and kind and love their stepchildren very much. Germaine did not have one of those stepmothers. Germaine had been born with one arm that was shorter and weaker than the other and had developed terrible sores on her neck and face. And so, if you can believe it, her wicked stepmother made the little girl sleep in the barn! She screamed at Germaine and hurt her and called her names. And when Germaine wanted to eat, she had to beg at the door until her stepmother either threw scraps of food at her or put some in the dog's bowl for her to eat.

I hope that if someone is treating you very badly, you will tell a grown-up. And if that grown-up doesn't fix the problem, I hope you will tell another grown-up and another and another until somebody helps you. God doesn't want you to be treated badly, he wants you to be loved and cherished. But Germaine didn't have anybody but God to help her, so she prayed—not that God would change her life, but that God would make her holy. She didn't want to become bitter or angry, but she knew that would take a miracle.

Germaine spent her days out in the fields watching her family's sheep and learning to love God better and better. Every day, she asked her guardian angel to watch the sheep so she could go to Mass. It worked! While the angel was on duty, her sheep never wandered, and no wolf ever attacked. And sometimes when she was running late, Germaine would walk right across the top of the river to get to Mass.

But Germaine's holiness wasn't just about miracles. She was patient and kind and generous, giving away her scraps of food to people who had even less than she did. Eventually Germaine's stepmother began to realize that Germaine was a miracle-worker; her greatest miracle was that she really did love her cruel stepmother. So when Germaine suddenly got sick and died, her stepmother went to Confession and became a good, kind woman. And St. Germaine Cousin, the holy little Cinderella, went home to Jesus to be a princess in heaven.

St. Germaine is on her way to Mass, preparing to receive Jesus as she leaves her flock of sheep behind in the charge of her guardian angel. You can see her limb difference and the scars from the scrofula that gave her sores.

Bl. Ghébrē-Michael

GUB-reh MEE-ka-yel
Ethiopia | 1791–1855
Feast Day: July 14

 Sometimes doing the right thing gets you branded a traitor. That's what happened to Bl. Ghébrē-Michael. He was born in Ethiopia, an African country that has been Christian for seventeen centuries. But for about sixteen centuries, the Ethiopian Church has been separated from the pope in Rome. That was the Church Ghébrē-Michael grew up in, the Church he loved, the Church he gave his life to as a monk.

Ghébrē-Michael had lost an eye in an accident when he was a child, which meant there were some jobs he couldn't do. But he could study and he could pray, which made being a monk the perfect vocation for him. Ghébrē-Michael was excited to spend his life growing in holiness with other men who wanted to be saints.

Unfortunately, that's not what Ghébrē-Michael found when he entered the monastery. The other monks didn't really want to pray or fast. They didn't want to fall in love with Jesus. When Ghébrē-Michael realized this, he was distraught! If even the men in the monastery didn't want to be holy, what hope was there for the Church and the world?

Ghébrē-Michael began to wonder why this was happening. Was it true of monks everywhere? So he started to research monasticism in Ethiopia and in other parts of the world. Then he began to travel to learn more. That's when he met St. Justin de Jacobis, a Catholic bishop whose hunger for holiness was so strong it made Ghébrē-Michael ask: what is it about the Catholic Church that made this man so holy? The more questions he asked, the more he knew: he had to be Catholic.

So Ghébrē-Michael became a Catholic, a scholar, a seminary professor, and eventually a priest. But his old friends didn't see that he was trying to get close to Jesus, they just saw that he had abandoned them, had gone over to a Church that they considered their enemy, though Catholics and Orthodox are really brothers and sisters in Jesus. Fr. Ghébrē-Michael was arrested and tortured and treated so badly that eventually he died because of it. His captors thought they had killed a traitor, but really they had made a martyr: Bl. Ghébrē-Michael, who wanted to be holy even if it meant he lost everything.

Bl. Ghébrē-Michael was a postulant in the Congregation of the Mission (Vincentians), who always wear the dress of local clergy, so he's dressed as he did when he was an Orthodox monk. After he was arrested, the emperor brought Ghébrē-Michael with him whenever he traveled. Ghébrē-Michael was so badly treated that he died on one of these journeys; the place of his death was not recorded except that it was under a cedar tree.

Bl. Hermann of Reichenau

HER-muhn of RYE-can-ow
Germany | 1013–1054
Feast Day: September 25

People called Bl. Hermann of Reichenau the wonder of his age. He was a genius. He wrote about math and astronomy, history and music theory. He studied theology and learned several languages. He even wrote about a complicated board game.

And he did all this with hands that could barely hold a pen and a speech impediment that made him difficult to understand. You see, Hermann had been born with a cleft palate and cerebral palsy and spinal muscular atrophy. He had a really hard time writing and an even harder time speaking. He was never going to be able to walk. And since he lived before wheelchairs were invented, any time he wanted to move to a different room he had to ask people to carry him.

But none of that stopped him.

When Hermann's parents realized how smart he was, they took him to a Benedictine abbey so that their brilliant son could learn. He lived there from the time he was seven, reading and writing and teaching and creating. He was the first European to build an astrolabe and a portable sundial. He wrote a book that told about the last thousand years of history.

Br. Hermann was happy to learn and to teach, but he continued to pray for healing, especially to Mary, who is the consoler of the afflicted. He knew she understood him in his suffering. One day, Our Lady appeared to him and asked if he would rather have health or wisdom. Br. Hermann must have been amazed to see her, but without a moment's hesitation, he chose wisdom—not for himself, but so that he could bless the world with his learning.

Br. Hermann's studies got harder toward the end of his life when he went blind. But in the darkness he began to compose music, some so beautiful we still sing it today, like the *Salve Regina* and the *Alma Redemptoris Mater*.

But holiness is even more important than genius. Br. Hermann was so smart he could have been arrogant. And he suffered so much it could have made him bitter. Instead, he was gentle, kind, and joyful. Because Bl. Hermann of Reichenau knew the love of God. He knew that God's love makes life worth living, whatever you have to offer the world.

Bl. Hermann's Brothers made him a special chair. We don't know exactly how it looked, but his disabilities likely would have meant he needed a headrest of some sort. He's holding a stylus to write on wax tablets. His astrolabe is hanging from his desk and his portable sundial from his armrest, while the hurdy-gurdy on the wall represents his musical contributions. Our Lady of Consolation (modeled on a fifth-century image) is appearing to him.

St. Hildegard of Bingen

HIL-duh-gard of BING-en
Germany | 1098–1179
Feast Day: September 17

 Hildegard of Bingen was absolutely brilliant, but for a long time she didn't quite believe it. Hildegard had been having visions of Jesus since she was three. At eight, she moved into an abbey to be raised and taught by nuns, and pretty soon became one herself. But even though Sr. Hildegard was tremendously clever and was figuring out all kinds of things about plants and medicines and music and theology, nobody had really taught her to write well in Latin. So Sr. Hildegard thought she probably shouldn't write down all the things she was learning. She didn't want people to laugh at her mistakes.

Sometimes the devil likes to tell you that lie: that you're not good enough or smart enough or pretty enough or strong enough or brave enough. God looks at you and says, "I love you so much and I made you exactly the way I wanted you!" But we can't always hear him telling us how much he loves us. And even though Sr. Hildegard knew how much God loved her, she still didn't think she was good enough to write. For years and years, she kept all her wisdom to herself until, when she was forty-two, God spoke right to her and told her she had to write.

Eventually, Sr. Hildegard got up the courage to be obedient, and it's a really good thing she did! Sr. Hildegard was already a mystic and a prioress (the nun in charge of the other nuns) and now she became a poet, composer, artist, playwright, pharmacist, and theologian, too. She wrote about Saints and medicine and natural history. Before too long, the pope had gotten ahold of her work and told everyone how great it was, which must have helped her believe in herself. And then he asked her to leave her abbey and travel around preaching—something nuns never, ever did. But Sr. Hildegard had learned to be obedient, so off she went for twelve years.

Sr. Hildegard eventually became so confident that she gave advice (and sometimes demands) to bishops, and an emperor, and even the pope! St. Hildegard of Bingen finally believed that God had made her good and wise and strong, and she used all her gifts to serve the Lord and his Church.

St. Hildegard is wearing her Benedictine habit, standing beside an illustration from her final great book of visions, Liber Divinorum Operum. *This book records ten mystical visions, including the one depicted here of the seasons of the year; the image can be found by searching for "Werk Gottes 12." Hildegard is holding a book and a quill and is illuminated by the light of God.*

St. Jacinta Marto

jah-SIN-tah MAR-to
Portugal | 1910–1920
Feast Day: February 20

When people first tried to make Jacinta Marto a Saint, the pope said no. He didn't think children were capable of "heroic virtue," which means doing the right thing even when it's hard. Well, you and I both know that's not true! Children can be very holy, even if it's hard.

Jacinta hadn't always wanted to be a Saint. Before Mary appeared to her, she had been pretty ordinary. She was sweet and liked to sing and dance, but she was also a little spoiled and had a bad habit of sulking if she didn't get her way. She loved Jesus, but she didn't much like to pray. In fact, when Jacinta, Francisco, and Lucia went out with their sheep, they prayed liked this:

Our Father, Hail Mary, Hail Mary,
Hail Mary, Hail Mary, Hail Mary,
Hail Mary, Hail Mary, Hail Mary,
Hail Mary, Hail Mary, Glory Be.

They did that five times and called it a Rosary. Can you imagine? But God can make a Saint out of absolutely anybody, and he sent his mother to the three children to call the world back to Jesus.

One day, they saw a beautiful lady, dressed in white and shining like the sun, who told them to pray and make sacrifices for the salvation of sinners. Lucia told Jacinta not to tell anyone yet. But Jacinta just couldn't help it! She told—

and everybody thought Jacinta, Francisco, and Lucia were lying. But they wouldn't deny Mary. Not when people made fun of them. Not when the priest yelled at them. Not even when the mayor put them in jail. They stayed faithful.

They saw Mary five times and saw the sun dance in the sky. And then it was all over and they had to choose to love God when everything was ordinary. Jacinta stopped sulking and started praying. For the rest of her short life, she made lots of little sacrifices, asking Jesus to save sinners.

St. Jacinta Marto died when she was nine. She's the youngest non-martyr ever to become a Saint, and it's not because Mary appeared to her. It's because even as a little girl she knew how to choose good and reject evil, how to love Jesus and offer him all her sufferings. It's because of heroic virtue, which every child is capable of.

St. Jacinta is standing with one of the lambs she was in charge of, looking at Our Lady of Fatima during an apparition. The halo behind Mary is a nod to the Miracle of the Sun, during which tens of thousands of people saw the sun dance in the sky at the last Fatima apparition. In her June apparition, Mary showed the children her heart, surrounded by the thorns of people's sins.

St. James Intercisus

James EEN-tare-CHEE-zoos
Iran | d. 421
Feast Day: November 27

D o you think God would still love you if you denied him? Of course he would! There is nothing, not one thing that you could do to make God stop loving you. But do you think he would make you a Saint after something like that? Well, he's done it before.

St. James Intercisus was a very important man. He was a soldier for the king of Persia and the king liked him an awful lot. That means he got money and power and all sorts of good things to eat. Before long James started to believe that those things were more important than Jesus. So when the king started persecuting Christians, James thought he had better pretend he wasn't one.

James pretended for a while, and it doesn't sound like he was even a little bit sorry. But his wife and his mother heard what had happened and they felt just awful. They were so worried about what would happen to James if he didn't repent! So when the king of Persia died, they wrote James a letter telling him that he had done something terribly wicked and that they were very concerned for his soul. They didn't yell and fuss and say he was a bad person. They just told him the truth: it was very wrong to deny Jesus.

James had managed to avoid thinking about this, but when he got the letter from his wife and mother, he couldn't ignore the truth anymore: he had done a dreadful thing and he needed to repent. But he knew he wasn't strong enough to be surrounded by riches and power again, so James stayed away, hoping that if he wasn't near temptation he wouldn't betray Jesus again.

The new king found out why James was gone, though. He called him back to court, demanding to know if James was a Christian. James had a choice to make. He could deny Jesus again and go back to his fancy and important life, or he could remember how God's mercy had saved him and be brave. When James proclaimed Jesus' name, the new king was very angry and very frightening. But God had strengthened St. James Intercisus, and the man who had been an apostate now had the courage to become a martyr and a Saint.

St. James is dressed in the uniform of an officer in the Sassanian army. He's standing in a typical Persian archway; the cross atop the dome (reminiscent of the ruins of the Rabban Hormizd Monastery in Iraq) reminds us that Christians have lived in Iran for many centuries, though they have often been persecuted.

St. Jerome

Slovenia, Palestine | 347–420
Feast Day: September 30

 Jerome was usually angry. And while it would be nice if I could say, "but then Jesus changed his heart and he became so sweet and patient," that's not what happened. St. Jerome was usually angry and then he died. He never stopped getting angry. But he never stopped fighting against his anger.

Jerome did a lot of amazing things in his life. He translated the Bible from Greek and Hebrew into Latin, making it possible for loads more people to read the Word of God. He was a monk. He was a spiritual director for many women, some of whom also became Saints. He served the poor. He wrote beautiful books and spent hours and hours in prayer.

But he never stopped losing his temper. And he never stopped repenting and trying to be better. That's what makes a Saint, after all: not that you never mess up, but that you always seek forgiveness. And Jerome was *always* asking for forgiveness. He wanted to be holy, he really did. It was just so hard.

There are lots of stories of Saints who were terribly wicked and then God made them holy. But I think it's nice to hear also about Saints who were only a little bit wicked and never managed to defeat their sin. It gives us hope when we make mistakes, knowing that plenty of Saints made a lot of mistakes, over and over again.

And maybe that's really what made Jerome a Saint. We can't know what kind of man he would have been if God had taken away his temper. Maybe he would have become proud or maybe he just would have settled into a mediocre life. But because Jerome kept sinning, he kept throwing himself at the feet of Jesus. And his repenting and repenting and repenting is what ended up making him so holy. That's what made this cranky old man, who some people called "the great name-caller," a Saint, and a good friend to all of us who get discouraged when we can't stop making the same mistake.

St. Jerome was a genius and a scholar and a spiritual father and a teacher, but most of all he was a sinner loved by God. Because you don't have to be perfect to be a Saint.

St. Jerome is sitting in the cave where he lived for thirty years in Bethlehem—the very same cave where tradition says Jesus was born. Legend has it that he tamed a lion in the wilderness by healing its paw, so he's usually shown with his lion friend. Because he was such an important priest in Rome, he's often depicted as a cardinal (even though this office didn't exist at the time), so he's wearing red here.

St. Joan of Arc

France | 1412–1431
Feast Day: May 30

How did a poor little girl from a tiny village end up leading the charge as the French army sought to liberate their country? Well, she prayed. And when she prayed, she listened.

Now, I'm not saying that if you listen in prayer, you'll hear the voices of St. Michael, St. Catherine of Alexandria, and St. Margaret of Antioch like Joan did. You might, of course. But even if you don't hear the voice of God (or his Saints) with your ears, when you sit with the Lord and make space for him in your heart, he begins to speak. He gives you a sense of what you ought to do, or he helps you to feel very sorry for your sins, or he fills you with joy in knowing his love.

To St. Joan of Arc, though, God spoke in words. And through her Saint friends, he told her that he needed her to help the French army. Can you imagine?

It took quite a while for Joan to convince the rich and powerful men in charge that she could be of any use, but she was filled with the Holy Spirit, and eventually she found herself riding at the head of the army as they went into battle. She hated the violence and ugliness of it all. Really, if it had been up to her, Joan would have stayed home with her mother. But she wanted to obey God, so Joan rode all around France praying and preaching and directing the men as they liberated their country. "I am not afraid," she said. "I was born for this."

More than anything, Joan helped soldiers to return to Jesus. Because of her words and her witness, many went to Confession and turned away from sin. That was the real miracle—all the battles won were nothing compared to the souls saved.

Eventually, Joan was captured by the enemy. They demanded that she confess that she had made up the story of the Saints speaking to her, but Joan refused. She hadn't wanted to go to war. She hadn't wanted to become a hero. She had only wanted to be faithful to God. And so St. Joan of Arc was killed, an ordinary girl who has inspired warriors for centuries just because she listened when she prayed.

St. Joan's hair is cut short because her heavenly voices instructed her to cut her long hair in the style most knights wore, and to wear men's clothes as she led her soldiers into battle. Her banner says "Jesus Mary" (in the spelling of the time) with an image of Christ the King being worshipped by two angels. There are fleurs-de-lys (a symbol of both the Catholic Church and France) decorating it.

St. John Colobus

John COLL-uh-bus
Egypt | 339–405
Feast Day: October 17

St. John Colobus wasn't always meek and obedient. But he wanted to be a saint, and he knew that he would have to let go of his own self-will if that was ever going to happen. So John Colobus (whose name means "John the Short") went to the desert to be a hermit, where he found an old man to be his spiritual father.

"Plant this walking stick in the ground and water it every day," the old hermit ordered him.

That is a crazy thing to do. What good could possibly come of watering an old, dead stick? Especially since the river was more than ten miles away! But John knew that holiness doesn't come from doing the pious things that we want to do, but from obeying the Lord. Even when he's speaking through other people. Even when his will sounds crazy.

Every day, John watered that stick. He walked ten miles to the river and ten miles back, just to pour some water on an old dead stick in the ground. Most days it must have felt like a giant waste of time—just like praying the Rosary can sometimes feel like a waste of time, or being kind to people who don't notice, or cleaning your room when it's just going to get dirty again. But John kept watering.

For three years, he watered that stick. And then, after three years, that old, dead stick sprouted leaves. And then flowers. And then fruit! John's spiritual father gave him a piece, saying, "Eat of the fruit of obedience."

John never did anything else spectacular. He obeyed and he ran away. When people made fun of him, he ran away so he wouldn't get angry. He even ran away when people got angry at each other. John knew that he wasn't holy enough to listen to people's bad language and bad attitudes without it messing up his language and his attitude. And so—by watering a stick and running from temptation—John became a Saint. Some of the hermits who lived nearby could work all kinds of miracles, but St. John Colobus's only real miracle was mastering his temper and learning to be obedient. And in the end, that kind of miracle is worth more than all the others put together.

St. John is carrying the jug he took to get water each day. The walking stick planted in front of him has borne fruit. We chose to portray it as a fig tree to stand in opposition to the fruitless fig tree Jesus cursed. You can see from the height of the walking stick that John was indeed quite short.

St. John Henry Newman

England | 1801–1890
Feast Day: October 9

Have you ever argued really, really hard for something and then suddenly realized you were wrong? And you had to decide if you were going to admit that you were wrong or just keep fighting to protect your pride? That's a hard situation to be in, and it's just where St. John Henry Newman was.

John Henry's family was Protestant (a kind of Christian who believes in Jesus but disagrees with the Catholic Church on some pretty big things). But he didn't really learn to love Jesus until he was fifteen. Unfortunately, the people who told him about Jesus also taught him that Catholics were very, very wrong. John Henry even believed that the pope was a tool of Satan! Still, he was coming to know God better and better and soon he decided to become an Anglican priest. He didn't exactly hate the Catholic Church anymore, but he sure didn't love it.

Once John Henry was an Anglican priest, he began to wonder why Anglicanism didn't look like the early Church. He argued that you could worship like Catholics worship and even believe what Catholics believe and still be Anglican. As long as you didn't follow the pope, he thought, it was okay! Pretty soon John Henry had lots of followers.

But the more he learned, the more John Henry understood that the Catholic Church was the Church founded by Jesus.

He tried to keep defending Anglicanism, but finally he realized that he had to become Catholic. Even though he would lose his job. Even though he would lose most of his friends. Even though all of England would think he was a traitor. And so, after many years of fighting against Catholicism, John Henry became a Catholic, then a Catholic priest, and eventually even a cardinal. And all the while, what he was telling everyone around him was, "I was wrong."

John Henry Cardinal Newman was a brilliant theologian. He wrote very important books and did very important work to help the Catholic Church in England, which had been persecuted for a long time. But none of that compared to the importance of admitting that he had been wrong. For some people, that takes more courage than walking into a lions' den, and for St. John Henry Newman, it's what made him a Saint.

St. John Henry is in the library at his home in Littlemore, Oxford. He's standing beside the desk where he wrote "An Essay on the Development of Christian Doctrine," which helped him convert to Catholicism. After Bl. Dominic Barberi received John Henry into the Church, Fr. Dominic used this desk as an altar for Mass; John Henry never wrote on it again. He's wearing a cardinal's attire, though he left Littlemore long before he became a cardinal.

Bl. John Sullivan

Ireland | 1861–1933
Feast Day: May 8

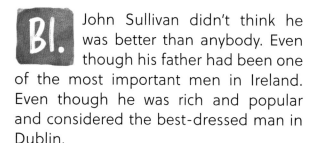 John Sullivan didn't think he was better than anybody. Even though his father had been one of the most important men in Ireland. Even though he was rich and popular and considered the best-dressed man in Dublin.

Well, maybe for a while he did. All the years that he was going on walking tours of Europe and working as a lawyer and impressing everybody with his good taste, he may have thought he was something special.

But then John went on a trip to Greece and spent time at an Orthodox monastery. Something about the way the monks lived—their simplicity, their prayer, their peace—tugged at John's heart. So when he got home, he left the Protestant faith he'd been ignoring for years and became a Catholic. Then John got rid of all his expensive things and began to live simply, giving everything he didn't need to the poor.

After that, John left behind his important job and his admiring friends and the fortune he'd inherited and went to study for the priesthood with eighteen-year-olds. But he didn't tell them how clever and important he'd been or look down on them for being young. He was just happy to learn.

After that, Mr. Popular became someone fairly ordinary. He was ordained a Jesuit priest and sent to teach at a school, where he discovered he wasn't a very good teacher. He wasn't a very good preacher, either. But Fr. John was good at loving people and listening to them, so he began to visit the poor and the sick, wearing his shabby cassock and riding the bicycle he had used for fun in his old life. And because he was so simple and so humble, God began to work miracles through Fr. John, one after another until people crowded around him whenever they could.

Still, Fr. John didn't think he was better than anyone. Once, another priest was annoyed to find Fr. John visiting one of his parishioners. Seeing that, Fr. John knelt on the floor to ask forgiveness. Can you imagine? But Fr. John didn't think he deserved any special attention, not because he used to be rich and important and not because he was a miracle-working priest. For Bl. John Sullivan, it was enough just to belong to God.

Bl. John is wearing a simple cassock. He has just left the home of a poor sick farmer living outside Dublin and is about to climb on the bicycle he'd ridden on his bike tours around Ireland when he was a fashionable young lawyer. Instead of racing other rich young men, Fr. John is on his way to hear Confessions, pray with the sick, or even work miracles.

St. Joseph Vaz

Joseph VAHZ
India, Sri Lanka | 1651–1711
Feast Day: January 16

Joseph Vaz was going to get to Sri Lanka if it was the last thing he did. He grew up in India, but as a young priest Fr. Joseph heard about the people of Sri Lanka. For nearly thirty years, there hadn't been a single priest there! Can you imagine? Thirty years with no Mass and no Confessions? Fr. Joseph was distraught—he asked to go there immediately.

He was sent instead to Eastern India. In obedience, he went, and worked there for three years, going everywhere barefoot so he could be like the poor. But his heart was set on Sri Lanka. Finally, he was given permission to go. Fr. Joseph put on a disguise, taking nothing with him but what he needed to say Mass, with sacred vessels hidden in pockets and tied around his waist. When he arrived, he had no money and had to beg door to door, all the while hiding from the Dutch Calvinists who had banned all priests from the territory they had captured.

As it turns out, the Dutch didn't notice him. They weren't expecting an Indian man to be a priest. But Fr. Joseph couldn't find any Catholics to serve—they were all in hiding. To find his flock, Fr. Joseph wore a rosary around his neck while begging at each door. People began to talk about him and finally one of the Catholics asked about his rosary. Fr. Joseph told the man that he was a priest. Just think how delighted they must have been! Imagine receiving Communion for the first time in thirty years. Or the first time in your life! Not one of the young people had ever been to Mass until Fr. Joseph came.

Fr. Joseph fled from one village to the next for four years, until he was captured as a spy and put on house arrest. But he earned the king's respect when he prayed for rain to end a drought and it began to pour—everywhere but right over Fr. Joseph, who stayed dry. After that, he was free to preach and serve throughout the kingdom. For twenty-four years, St. Joseph Vaz preached the Gospel, an adopted son of Sri Lanka just as much as he was an adopted son of God.

St. Joseph is wearing a rosary around his neck, always seeking persecuted Catholics to minister to even while proclaiming the Gospel by preaching the Cross to non-Christians. This image shows the miracle that earned the respect of the King of Kandy, when rain poured around him to end a drought while Fr. Joseph remained dry.

St. Josephine Bakhita

JOE-suh-FEEN bah-KEE-ta
Sudan, Italy | 1869–1947
Feast Day: February 8

St. Josephine Bakhita knew how to forgive. And it's a good thing, because a lot of people had hurt her. When she was only seven she was kidnapped and sold into slavery. The wicked men who stole her told her that she wasn't really a person, that she didn't matter. Now, was that true? Of course not! Josephine was good and important, even when everybody said she wasn't.

But it wasn't until many years later, when she was given a crucifix, that Josephine heard for the first time that God loved her and died to save her. You can imagine how glad she was to hear that! And when she looked at poor Jesus who had suffered so much, she understood that he had been with her during all the years she had been enslaved.

After that, Josephine knew she had to be baptized. So when her owners told her it was time to leave Italy, she refused. "I'm not going anywhere until I've been baptized."

Well, her owners yelled. And they threatened. And then they called the police who called the judge who decided they had to let Josephine go! Once she was free, all Josephine really wanted was to join the Sisters who had told her how wildly God loved her. So she did, and she spent her life cooking meals and answering the door.

Sr. Josephine wanted to be simple and ignored, but for years she was told to travel and tell her story. When people heard it, they felt awfully sorry for Sr. Josephine. But she kept telling them that hers wasn't a sad story. It was a story of God bringing so much good out of such evil. She said that if she met the people who had kidnapped her, "I would kneel and kiss their hands, for if that had not happened, I would not be a Christian and a religious today."

Now that doesn't mean Sr. Josephine thought that those wicked men had done a good thing—not at all! It means that she had forgiven them. She didn't hate them. Can you imagine forgiving someone who had hurt you that badly? But St. Josephine Bakhita knew that Jesus had forgiven her and she was willing to forgive absolutely anyone because she was so, so glad to belong to him.

St. Josephine is wearing the habit of the Canossian Sisters and gazing on the crucifix. Behind her is a memory of her childhood in slavery, reaching for the beauty that spoke to her of God. She later said, "Seeing the sun, the moon and the stars, I said to myself, 'Who could be the Master of these beautiful things?' And I felt a great desire to see him, to know him and to pay him homage."

St. Juan Diego Cuauhtlatoatzin

HWAN dee-EH-go
KWAH-ooh-TLAH-toe-AHT-seen
Mexico | 1474–1548
Feast Day: December 9

C enturies ago, in a land where the people wanted nothing to do with Jesus, a miracle happened. This miracle was so amazing that eight million people became Catholic in the next seven years—the biggest number of conversions in the history of the world. And all because of an old farmer's coat.

When the first missionaries had come to Mexico, St. Juan Diego Cuauhtlatoatzin and his wife had been among the few Aztecs who wanted to become Catholic. Seven years later, Juan Diego was walking to Mass early one December morning when he heard heavenly music and saw the most beautiful woman he'd ever seen, an Aztec woman dressed like a princess. The Lady called Juan Diego by name and told him something astonishing: she was the Virgin Mary, the Mother of God. "I am your merciful mother," she told him, "the merciful mother of all who live in this land."

What an amazing message! Mary had come looking like Juan Diego, speaking to him and to all his people, to say that she wasn't just the mother of the Spanish soldiers and missionaries but of the Aztecs as well. She loved them!

Then Mary asked Juan Diego to convince the bishop to build a chapel in her honor. Juan Diego didn't think the bishop would listen, and he was right. The bishop needed proof. So a few days later, Mary filled Juan Diego's cloak with roses. Roses in the middle of winter! Surely this was the sign the bishop was waiting for.

But when Juan Diego opened his cloak to show the roses, the bishop fell on his knees, staring not at the roses but at the cloak. There, on Juan Diego's old cactus-fiber cloak, was a beautiful image of Mary, her face and clothes like an Aztec princess's. The bishop was amazed and so were the people. If the Mother of God had given them such a sign, surely she must be their mother, too. And so Mexico became one of the most Catholic countries in the world, full of people who love Our Lady of Guadalupe and are so thankful for St. Juan Diego Cuauhtlatoatzin, an old farmer who helped them learn that the Mother of God was their mother, too.

St. Juan Diego's tilma is full of Castilian roses, which grew only in the bishop's home country of Spain. Mary stands above him, dressed as an Aztec princess, clothed with the sun, with the moon under her feet (Rev 12:1). The position of her sash tells us that she is pregnant and the stars on her cloak mirror the position of the stars in the sky that night.

St. Kaleb the Ethiopian

Ethiopia | d. 540
Feast Day: May 15

Have you ever done the right thing for all the wrong reasons? That's what the warrior-king of Axum did, and it got him into a lot of trouble.

St. Kaleb the Ethiopian had heard that a king in Arabia had killed hundreds of Christians. He was so angry about it that he went flying off in a rage to punish that wicked king. He rode into battle thinking that he would win easily with God on his side. But when he was defeated, King Kaleb didn't know what to think. He went to visit an old monk to ask his advice.

"Why did you fight that battle?" the old monk asked.

"To protect innocent Christians!" the king cried.

"That's why you said you fought it. Why did you really fight it?"

Suddenly, King Kaleb realized that he hadn't really gone into battle to defend people. He had gone because he was angry. He had gone because he was proud. He wanted his enemy punished and *he* wanted to be the one to do it.

King Kaleb knew that wasn't right. He begged God to forgive him and went back to his soldiers, ready to use his power to protect people, not to hurt them.

Again they rode out to battle, and this time King Kaleb was successful. He won the war and made sure that Christians in that area would be safe for years to come.

But when he got home, he knew he had to change. Some people can be holy while having power and money, but King Kaleb was not one of those people.

So he trained his son to be a holy Christian king, and then Kaleb took off his crown and headed into the desert to pray. He left behind riches and comfort and found God in silence and poverty instead. He prayed and fasted, and pretty soon God made him so holy that he began to work miracles, too. For the rest of his life, St. Kaleb the Ethiopian lived in the desert, a warrior-king turned miracle-working hermit who now did the right things for all the right reasons.

St. Kaleb is wearing patterns inspired by medieval Ethiopian artwork. To his right is a castle modeled on re-creations of the ruins at Dungur, an ancient mansion in the capital city of Aksum. The obelisks were built in pre-Christian Ethiopia as monuments to the dead. Kaleb is turning from power, wealth, and honor to face the mountain of Debre Damo, atop which is a sixth-century monastery which can only be reached by a rope ladder.

St. Kateri Tekakwitha

KAT-ur-ee TEK-ak-WITH-ah
(It's commonly pronounced kah-TARE-ee or kah-TEER-ee, but KAT-ur-ee is more accurate)
United States, Canada, Mohawk Nation | 1656–1680
Feast Day: July 14

Nobody thought St. Kateri Tekakwitha was worth much. She was the daughter of the Mohawk chief and his Christian Algonquin wife, but by the time she was four, Kateri's mom and dad and brother had all died of smallpox, a frightful disease that dimmed Kateri's eyesight and scarred her face.

People thought she was ugly and a burden. They made fun of her for being clumsy. Even her name was a mean joke. They called her "she who bumps into things" (Tekakwitha) because she couldn't see very well. Her uncle had taken her to live with him, but he didn't believe in Jesus. He made fun of Kateri for praying. When she rested on Sundays, the other villagers wouldn't let her eat. And when she went away by herself to pray, they told lies about her and said she was meeting a boy in the woods.

Kateri could have decided to become bitter and hate the people who were so cruel to her. Or she could have given up on Jesus instead of trying to be the only Christian in her village. But Kateri's mom had told her about Jesus when she was little, and she knew how much God loved her. He had never abandoned her and she wouldn't abandon him.

When Kateri was eleven, missionaries came to her village, and she was able to start learning more and more about Jesus. She decided she wanted never to marry but to belong only to Jesus—which caused her even more problems in the village. And all this time, Kateri hadn't even been allowed to be baptized!

She was finally baptized when she was twenty. After that, her people were so un-kind that she decided to run away to a Christian village. She left behind every-one she loved and journeyed hundreds of miles through the wilderness, stumbling often because of her weak eyes. When she finally arrived, Kateri heard for the first time that she wasn't ugly and weak and stupid and lazy. She had always known that God thought she was wonderful, but now she had friends who knew it, too. And more than that—they thought she was holy and marvelous. When St. Kateri Tekakwitha died a few years later, she was finally surrounded by people who knew what she was worth.

St. Kateri is standing beside one of the crosses she built in the forest as a little chapel. Her clothes are based on a painting by Fr. Claude Chauchetière, a Jesuit priest who was with her when she died and advocated for her canonization. Behind her is the St. Lawrence River and a boat like the one she took to her Christian village. The turtle represents her membership in the Turtle clan of the Mohawks.

St. Katharine Drexel

Katharine DREX-el
United States | 1858–1955
Feast Day: March 3

 Katharine Drexel gave up a seven-million-dollar fortune—which would be two hundred million dollars today—to serve the people everyone else ignored.

Katharine was raised in the lap of luxury by parents who loved Jesus and loved the poor. From the time she was little, Katharine was used to helping her stepmother serve needy people at their home three days a week. So it was no great surprise that the little heiress thought she might be called to religious life. But nobody was at all sure that Katharine could handle it. After years and years of living how she liked, they thought life in a convent would be too hard.

Then Katharine went on a trip out West. Seeing the suffering of Native Americans left her desperately worried about how the Church could serve them. She was so worried, she went to speak to the pope about it, asking him to send missionaries to serve Native Americans. But the pope said, "You go."

At first, Katharine wasn't sure she was holy enough, but the Holy Spirit kept tugging, so she left everything behind and handed herself over as the servant of Black and Native American people.

Philadelphia society was shocked. One of the richest, most eligible girls in the country was leaving behind an enormous fortune to serve people they hardly thought were human. It was unthinkable. But Katharine didn't care. She founded an order to do the incredibly important work of serving people who were usually ignored, even by the Church. For nearly fifty years, Mother Katharine traveled all around the United States, founding convents and schools—fifty schools for African Americans and twelve for Native Americans.

And all the while, Mother Katharine was fighting racism and unjust laws that made her work nearly impossible. People threatened to hurt the Sisters. Once they even burned one of the Sisters' schools down. But Mother Katharine didn't quit. People were suffering, and she would work and serve and write letters and fight for changes in the law until everybody was treated equally.

St. Katharine Drexel's work still isn't done. People are still treated unjustly because of how they look or where their ancestors came from. But when we work for justice, we do it with an intercessor who gave up everything to do the same.

St. Katharine is wearing the habit of the Sisters of the Blessed Sacrament. She first realized how Black and Native American people struggled when she was a young woman on a train trip out West with her family. When she founded her community, she vowed to serve Black and Native American people. After that, she spent much of her life riding on trains to work with them in the religious houses and schools she'd founded across America.

St. Kuriakose Elias Chavara

KOO-ree-ah-kohss el-EE-as
CHA-vah-rah
India | 1805–1871
Feast Day: January 3

What would you do if someone told you a whole group of people weren't really people? That they didn't deserve rights and couldn't be taught to read? That you ought to treat them like garbage?

I hope you would refuse. Even if it made people mad, I hope you would work hard to help hurting people feel loved. That's just what St. Kuriakose Elias Chavara did. He lived in a time when a whole group of people were called "untouchables" (or Dalits) because other people had decided they were worthless. He didn't set out to change that at first. He just wanted to follow Jesus. But you'll find that if you give your life to Jesus, he does far more with it than you would ever have dreamed.

Kuriakose belonged to the Syro-Malabar Church, an Indian Catholic Church that began when the Apostle St. Thomas preached the Gospel in India. When he grew up, Kuriakose became a priest and began to realize how much the Dalit people in his community suffered. So much of their struggle was because they were poor. Without an education, Fr. Kuriakose knew most of them would stay poor. It was illegal to teach Dalits, but Fr. Kuriakose didn't care. He founded schools that would welcome them, the first in all of India. He saw that more children would come to school if they were fed there, so he began to offer free lunch. The Indian government realized what a good idea this was, and now all public schools in India do the same. And when Fr. Kuriakose became important in his diocese, he made a rule that all the churches had to have a school and they all had to teach Dalit children. He built schools for girls, too, even when people thought women didn't need an education. Now one hundred percent of the people in his region can read, all because of Fr. Kuriakose!

Fr. Kuriakose wrote theology, plays, and poetry. He founded two religious orders. He started the first newspaper in his native language. But St. Kuriakose Elias Chavara will always be remembered as the man who fought for the rights of people who were considered nothing. That's a legacy worth remembering.

St. Kuriakose is wearing his Carmelite habit and standing outside his childhood home in Kainakary. His hands are together in a traditional greeting honoring the dignity of the person you're encountering; the Dalits he served would never before have received this greeting from someone of Fr. Kuriakose's status, but he always treated them with dignity. Fr. Kuriakose sent mango tree seedlings to monasteries around India; this variety became known as the Prior Mango in his honor.

Bl. Ladislaus Bukowinski

LOD-iss-LOSS BOO-ko-VEENG-skee
Poland, Kazakhstan | 1904–1974
Feast Day: June 20

Bl. Ladislaus Bukowinski thanked God that he was arrested for no good reason and sent to a prison camp to work in the mines for ten hours every day. It turns out that's exactly where he needed to be.

Fr. Ladislaus had been a priest in Poland for ten years when he found himself in a communist prison camp with guards shooting into the crowd. But instead of ducking and covering, he crawled around absolving people's sins as they lay dying. When he got out of the camp, the Nazis were in charge, but Fr. Ladislaus didn't even try to protect himself. Instead, he began his mission of smuggling people to safety, especially Jewish children.

When the Nazis were pushed out, Fr. Ladislaus was arrested again by the communists. This time, he was sent to work in the copper mines of Kazakhstan, where he had to celebrate Mass in secret (using his bed as an altar) and pray a Rosary with beads made of old bread. After ten years, he was finally free to serve as a priest—the only active priest in all Kazakhstan!

You would think that when Fr. Ladislaus was told he could go home to Poland he would have jumped at the chance. But he trusted that God was at work in his exile in Kazakhstan. "Divine Providence sometimes works through atheists," he said, "who sent me there, where a father was needed."

Fr. Ladislaus traveled all around Kazakhstan and even to Tajikistan, trying to avoid the notice of the communist police. And people came to him, too, sometimes traveling nearly two hundred miles just so they could go to Mass. Imagine wanting to go to Mass so badly that you would travel that far, all the while risking your life!

Eventually, Fr. Ladislaus was worn out by all his years in labor camps and all his years on the run. But he wasn't a bit sorry for how his life had gone. He knew that God had used the wicked men who had arrested and imprisoned him. They were trying to do evil, but God had worked it all for good, sending Bl. Ladislaus Bukowinski just where he was needed. And trusting that God was directing his life (even when it sure didn't look that way)—well, that had changed everything.

Bl. Ladislaus is celebrating a clandestine Mass in his home in Karaganda, while a communist police officer walks past his window. His suitcase is on the floor, prepared for one of his many trips into Tajikistan; his mug shot (which can be seen online) is shown like a wanted poster. The picture of the Madonna and Child behind him is from his apartment; it's a Glykophilousa ("Sweet-kissing" or "Loving Kindness"), in which baby Jesus comforts his mother.

St. Laura Montoya

Laura mon-TOY-ah
Colombia | 1874–1949
Feast Day: October 21

Everyone thought St. Laura Montoya was crazy. To go out into the jungle? With no men to protect her? To serve the Indigenous people? To live the way they lived, with dirt floors and no running water? And treat them *like they were people*? She was clearly nuts.

But Laura knew what it was like to feel rejected and alone. Her father had died when she was little and she'd gone to live with a grandmother who always made Laura feel unwanted. Then Laura was sent to an orphanage. She went to a very good school, but felt as though she didn't belong there any more than she belonged with her own family.

So when she became a teacher, Laura had a heart for children who felt unloved, especially the Indigenous children who were treated so badly. She was praying for them one day when suddenly she knew that God was asking her to be a mother to them.

And soon Laura realized why God hadn't called her to be a cloistered nun, as she'd wanted. It wasn't just that she was loud and active and fun—nuns can be all of those things. It was that he wanted to send her to people who didn't yet know his love. So Laura and some other ladies went off into the jungle to serve, even though everybody thought they were quite peculiar. Women had never before gone out as missionaries like this. What were they doing, women by themselves? Did they hate men? How could they help the Native people? And why would they want to? Everyone thought these people were no better than animals.

But Laura knew that Jesus loved the Indigenous people. He'd made her a mother to them so they didn't have to live without him. And so that he could love them well, he'd started this crazy new religious order. Mother Laura spent twenty-five years living with the Native people, eating what they ate and never looking down on them for their customs. Eventually she wasn't able to travel through the jungle anymore, so she spent ten years in a wheelchair, writing letters (and over thirty books) and loving her children from a distance. People didn't think St. Laura Montoya was so crazy anymore—and now they know she's a Saint.

St. Laura is wearing the habit of the Missionary Sisters of the Immaculate Virgin Mary and Saint Catherine of Siena. The ants are a nod to a childhood mystical experience when she was helping ants move leaves and was overwhelmed by God's presence. The snake represents a vision she had of dangerous animals who could hurt her Sisters; God told her not to be afraid, and none of the Sisters were ever hurt by a wild animal.

Bl. Laurentia Herasymiv

loh-REN-tsee-ah hair-AHS-ee-miv
Ukraine, Russia | 1911–1952
Feast Day: August 26

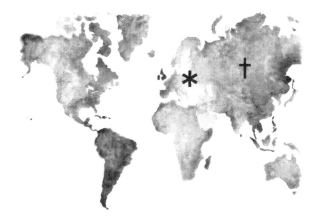

Sometimes being a martyr isn't the hardest part.

When Bl. Laurentia Herasymiv entered a Byzantine Catholic convent at nineteen, she knew her life wouldn't be simple: Ukraine was not a safe place for Catholics. And when Sr. Laurentia and her Sisters wouldn't turn their backs on the pope and become Orthodox instead of Catholic, the communists began to target them. They broke into the convent one night, scaring poor Sr. Laurentia so much she climbed out the window and hid in a bush for the whole rainy night.

Sr. Laurentia got sick after that and never really felt better again. But when the Sisters were arrested, the guards didn't care that she was sick. She still had to sleep on the concrete floor and go without food for days. She still had to go on a long, freezing train ride to Siberia, a dreadfully cold part of Russia. And though she went with her Sister, Bl. Olympia Bida, the journey was very hard. Then, when they arrived in Siberia, they had nowhere to live—nobody wanted to take in someone as sick as Sr. Laurentia.

The only place Sr. Laurentia could live was in a room with a very ill man who used to moan and shout. His pain had made him impatient, so he could be cruel. I don't know about you, but I think that might have been the last straw for me. To be persecuted and exiled while sick and exhausted, to be taunted and rejected, and then to be stuck in a room with a loud and rude man who didn't even care how sick I was? I think I might have been done accepting my cross.

But Sr. Laurentia didn't shout at the sick man. She didn't even complain about him. She loved him and she prayed for him. She took her sufferings and offered them to Jesus, even when it was hard. And through her prayer and her joy, her room-mate changed. He became kinder and more joyful. Joy does that, you know—it spreads.

Sr. Laurentia got sicker and sicker, but suffered most because there was no priest to give her the last sacraments. Still, when she died Bl. Laurentia Herasymiv knew Jesus was close to her. After long years of suffering well for him, dying as a martyr wasn't so hard after all.

Bl. Laurentia is wearing the religious habit of the Sisters of St. Joseph. She has a blanket wrapped around her to keep out the biting cold of Siberia and a rosary clutched in her hand as she clung to Jesus. Behind her is the train that carried her to the land where she died.

Bl. Leonid Feodorov

LAY-oh-NID FYOE-dore-off
Russia | 1879–1935
Feast Day: March 7

Bl. Leonid Feodorov had a problem. He had always loved Jesus, always wanted to be a priest. When he was finally old enough, Leonid kissed his mother goodbye and went off to seminary.

But he couldn't stop thinking about how Jesus had made Peter the pope. You see, Leonid wasn't a Catholic. He belonged to the Orthodox Church, which believes almost everything Catholics do but doesn't follow the pope. Leonid had never questioned that, but suddenly he began to wonder how the Church could stay true to Jesus without being led by the Holy Father.

Pretty soon Leonid knew he had to become Catholic, even though it was illegal. He snuck out of Russia, made up a fake name to hide from the secret police, and became Catholic. But though he had become a Roman Catholic, Leonid soon realized that to help bring the Russian people into the Church, he had to be a Byzantine Catholic, to pray in Russian and worship as his people did. So Leonid was ordained a Byzantine priest and prepared to go back to Russia.

Fr. Leonid knew he could be sent to prison. But he wanted to help his people be reunited to the Catholic Church, and he wanted to be obedient to God, so off he went. Just as soon as he got to Russia,

he was arrested and sent to Siberia, to be freezing and famished and exhausted in a prison camp. After he got out, he was put in charge of the Russian Byzantine Church. This made him the enemy of the communists, who hated all religion and sent Fr. Leonid back to prison.

Fr. Leonid could have sulked. But instead he and the other Byzantine priests worked with the Roman Catholic priests to worship together in secret. Their whole day revolved around being with Jesus in the Eucharist, no matter how risky it was. And the Orthodox people saw how there was no division between Roman Catholics and Byzantine Catholics, all because of their deep love of Jesus in the Eucharist.

Finally, Fr. Leonid was set free, but it was too late. His years of suffering had weakened his body and Bl. Leonid Feodorov died at only fifty-five, a martyr whose only strength had come from the Eucharist.

Bl. Leonid is dressed in a Soviet prisoner's uniform, standing beside the train tracks that ran through the barren landscape of Siberia, where he was initially imprisoned in Tobolsk. He's holding the spoon and chalice that are used for Communion during the Byzantine liturgy; he wouldn't have had such beautiful vessels in prison, but they symbolize his love of the Eucharist and of his Byzantine Catholic faith.

St. Leopold Mandić

LEE-uh-pold MAHN-deech
Montenegro, Italy | 1866–1942
Feast Day: July 30

St. Leopold Mandić never got what he wanted.

Oh, he got a lot of things he wanted. But he had one dream, one life-long ache that was never fulfilled. Leopold wanted to reunite the Church. Nearly one thousand years earlier, there had been a big split (a schism) between Christians in the West, who were called Catholics and followed the pope, and Christians in the East, who were called Orthodox and didn't. And Leopold was certain that God wanted to use him to help end that schism.

So Leopold became a Capuchin priest. But his voice wasn't very strong and neither was his health. Arthritis had stunted his growth so he was only four feet, five inches tall and he had a weak stomach and weak eyes. His superiors thought he would do a better job hearing Confessions than stuttering to crowds, so they sent him to Italy.

There are almost no Orthodox Christians in Italy. But Fr. Leopold had vowed to be obedient, so he went. Still, he kept going back to his superiors, reminding them, "I really do think God is calling me to work to reunite the Church." "Go back to the confessional," they would answer.

So Fr. Leopold heard Confessions. For fifteen hours a day he heard Confessions and for four hours a night, he stayed up and prayed. And while he didn't get to bring millions of Christians back to the Church, he consoled himself that every Confession he heard was a little piece of that big work. And he was happy.

Finally, Fr. Leopold's superiors called him in. "Pack your bags!" they cried. "We're sending you to the East!" Fr. Leopold was so excited! After decades of hoping and dreaming and praying, he was finally going to get to do the work he was made to do.

But when people in his town found out, they practically rioted. Fr. Leopold hadn't been in Croatia a week when his superiors told him to come back.

Fr. Leopold obeyed. He spent the rest of his life hearing Confessions in Italy. He died never having accomplished his heart's deepest desire. But he died a happy man, because he died faithful to the God he loved. St. Leopold Mandić became a Saint through disappointment and failure because he loved Jesus more than he loved himself.

St. Leopold is wearing his Capuchin habit and a purple stole to hear the Confessions of the many people waiting in line to be reconciled to God. Even standing up, he's shorter than his kneeling penitents. He's holding the cane he used because of his arthritis.

St. Lorenzo Ruiz

lo-REN-zo roo-EESS
Philippines, Japan | 1594–1637
Feast Day: September 28

St. Lorenzo Ruiz's life was out of control.

At first, it wasn't. He grew up in a Catholic family in the Philippines. He was an altar server and became a calligrapher, writing out important documents for people in his best handwriting. He got married and had three kids. He loved Our Lady of the Rosary and Marian processions. Life was pretty good.

Then things started to go wrong. A Spanish man had killed someone, and the Spanish authorities decided to blame Lorenzo. Lorenzo knew that if it was his word against a Spaniard's, the court would never believe a Filipino-Chinese man. Even though he hadn't done anything wrong, Lorenzo had a choice: he could let these lying men arrest him and kill him just because of his race, or he could leave his family behind and run away to save his life.

Lorenzo ran. He went to the Dominicans, who snuck him onto a ship leaving the country. Lorenzo heaved a huge sigh of relief. He was headed to Macao, in China. He would be far from his family, but he could get a job and send for them. Everything was going to be okay.

But the boat went to Okinawa instead, an island ruled by a Japanese government that hated Christians. Lorenzo must have been pretty upset when he found out the danger he was headed into! But what could he do? He went with the missionaries—and was captured with them almost immediately. Here was an ordinary man just trying to survive, and suddenly he was being asked to be a martyr. Staying safe wasn't an option anymore. He could lose his soul or he could lose his life.

For two years, Lorenzo struggled in prison. Sometimes the guards hurt him so badly that he thought about denying Jesus. But God's grace is bigger than our weakness, and Our Lady of the Rosary held him strong. In the end, brave Lorenzo told his torturers, "Even if I had a thousand lives, I would offer them all to God."

God had been working through all the craziness of Lorenzo's out-of-control life. One bad thing had led to another and another—which had all led to a martyr's crown and a place in heaven. And St. Lorenzo Ruiz knew it was all worth it.

St. Lorenzo is standing on the shore in the Philippines, clinging to his rosary and bracing himself against the winds of change. The palm trees to his right foretell his martyrdom, as palm leaves are a symbol of martyrdom. Behind him is the ship that will take him not to safety but to death.

St. Macrina the Younger

mah-CREE-na the Younger
Turkey | 330–379
Feast Day: July 19

St. Macrina the Younger's brothers are Saints. Her sister is a Saint. Her parents are Saints. Her grandmother is a Saint. That is a lot of holy people in one family! But Macrina isn't a Saint just because everyone around her was holy—if anything, it was the other way around.

Macrina was the oldest and helped to raise her little siblings, but it was when they were grown that they really needed her. St. Basil the Great, her biggest brother, had gone off to school and come home thinking he was just marvelous. Macrina was proud of how clever her brother was, but she was worried about what would happen to him with that attitude. So she sat him down and encouraged him to leave behind the things of this world and to live for God alone. Because of Macrina, Basil became a bishop and is now a Doctor of the Church.

The same thing happened with St. Gregory of Nyssa, who came home from school more interested in learning than in Jesus. But Macrina was a good big sister and before long, Gregory was a bishop, too. Bishop Gregory thought Macrina was so wonderful that he wrote several books about her, including one where she was the teacher, explaining all about death and the soul.

After her father died, Macrina basically raised her youngest brother, St. Peter of Sebaste, who also went on to become a bishop. They were so close that when Macrina founded a community of nuns, Bishop Peter helped direct the men's community that grew up next door. She's even the reason her mother is a Saint! St. Emilia had been living a pretty ordinary life, when Macrina encouraged her to give away her wealth and begin living for heaven.

Do you think anybody would have listened to Macrina if she had been bossy or cruel? If she had been selfish or lazy? No, Macrina was a good big sister because she loved her brothers and sisters the way they deserved to be loved. Because she respected them and treated them with kindness. And when a Saint lives like that, people around her become Saints. St. Macrina the Younger might be the world's best big sister, and loving her family well helped most of them become Saints, too.

St. Macrina is shown here as a patient (but amused) teacher. She's surrounded by her holy family. Clockwise from bottom left are Theosebia (sister), Peter of Sebaste (brother), Gregory of Nyssa (brother), Macrina the Elder (grandmother), Basil the Elder (father), Emilia (mother), Basil the Great (brother), and Naucratios (brother). Theosebia and Naucratios are considered Saints in the Orthodox Church; the others are all revered in the Catholic Church as well.

St. Margaret of Castello

Margaret of cah-STEL-oh
Italy | 1287–1320
Feast Day: April 13

Poor St. Margaret of Castello. Her parents thought she should never have been born. They were fancy people who wore fancy clothes and had fancy friends and they were *not interested* in a baby who wasn't perfect.

And while Margaret was good and loveable, she sure didn't look perfect. She was blind. One of her legs was longer than the other, her spine was curved, and she only ever grew to be four feet tall. So Margaret's parents decided to pretend their sweet, joyful, disabled daughter didn't exist.

For years they ignored her. Finally, they took her to another town and abandoned her without even telling her they were leaving.

Can you imagine? Poor Margaret had never been out of her hometown, and now she was alone in a strange place and couldn't even see to know what was happening.

Margaret would have had every right to be furious with her parents. But she forgave them. Because she knew something they didn't know: she was loved. It was good that she existed. God loved her blind eyes and her uneven walk and her short body. He loved everything about her. And it hurt that her parents didn't, but Margaret wasn't going to let that get in the way of loving God.

At first, Margaret became a beggar. But soon people began to see the joy and love and kindness that made Margaret so beautiful. They realized that she was holy. Once word got out, some nuns decided Margaret really ought to come live with them, because they were awfully holy, too.

It turns out that people who talk about how holy they are usually aren't. And when Margaret wouldn't gossip with them or skip prayers with them or waste time with them, those nuns made fun of her, spread lies about her, and finally kicked her out onto the street!

But Margaret forgave them, too, because she knew the truth: God loved her like crazy. She spent the rest of her life living in people's homes, serving the sick and the dying and teaching children, in between hours and hours of prayer—during which she sometimes levitated! St. Margaret of Castello was little, but her heart for God was huge and her love for him showed all the world how very good it was that she had been born.

St. Margaret was a third order Dominican, so she's wearing a Dominican habit. You can see that Margaret is a little person, that she's blind and has legs of different lengths and uses a cane, but her enormous smile is her most striking feature (to us and to the child Margaret is delighting in).

Bl. Margaret Pole

England | 1473–1541
Feast Day: May 28

When Bl. Margaret Pole was little, her aunt was the queen of England. When Margaret got older, her cousin became the queen. By the time she was grown, she was married to the king's cousin and had become lady-in-waiting to a princess.

It sounds very glamorous, doesn't it? But fancy clothes and titles don't always add up to a happy life, and Margaret's life was often very hard. Her mother had died when she was a little girl, her father was executed for treason, and she and her brother were often little better than prisoners. Then, when things had finally gotten easier and she was the happy mother of five children, her husband died and she found herself with no money and no home.

But soon Margaret's fortunes changed. Her cousin's little boy had become king, and she was given a title and lands and money. Before long, Countess Margaret was one of the richest people in England. She was godmother to the king's oldest child and the king himself called her "the saintliest woman in Christendom." Life was good.

But things were about to get very complicated for Catholics in England. King Henry VIII had decided to make himself head of the Church in England, and people who weren't willing to turn their backs on the pope were being killed for it.

It would have been so easy for Margaret to go along with Henry. She had suffered so much—didn't she have a right to hang on to the comfortable life she'd made for herself? But Margaret knew it wasn't right for Henry to make all the Christians in England leave the Church founded by Jesus. She didn't fight the king or tell all the world he was wrong. She just quietly went away. And when her sons took a stand against Henry and got arrested, Margaret stood with them and fell with them. She didn't beg for her life when she was arrested, or lie about her beliefs. She didn't shout that Henry was wicked or even cry out the name of Jesus. Bl. Margaret Pole just went quietly to win the crown of martyrdom, no longer a countess but a queen among women.

Bl. Margaret is standing in her room in the Tower of London. There is one portrait that is traditionally considered to be her, so she's dressed in clothes and jewelry inspired by that painting. Many of the windows in the Tower were cross-shaped, from the time when they were used by archers. After her death, a poem was found on the wall of her cell, likely written there by Margaret. The last line is found here.

Bl. María Antonia de Paz y Figueroa

ma-REE-a ahn-TONE-ya deh
PAHSS ee FEE-gay-ROE-ah |
Mama Antula: MAH-mah ahn-TOO-lah
Argentina | 1730–1799
Feast Day: March 7

 Did you know that sometimes to be obedient to God you have to be a rebel? Bl. María Antonia de Paz y Figueroa was a rebel, though she never set out to be. She was raised rich and fancy, but when she was just fifteen she made vows to live in poverty and belong only to Jesus. Eventually, she even founded a community of women religious to help in her work. And the people loved her so much they began to call her by a nickname—Mama Antula—which is what everybody still calls her today.

Mama Antula loved the Spiritual Exercises, a retreat led by the Jesuits where you use your imagination to learn to love Jesus better. But one day the King of Spain kicked every single Jesuit out of his territory. There was nobody left to lead the Spiritual Exercises—so Mama Antula decided to do it herself.

Mama Antula started wandering all over Argentina leading retreats. And she did it barefoot! She became so famous that in the twenty years she was preaching, one hundred thousand people came on retreat with her: beggars and Spanish nobles and priests and Native farmers and enslaved people and bishops. Everybody came.

Well, not everybody. Actually, a lot of people thought a woman had no business telling people how to pray. They said Mama Antula was crazy, or even wicked. They thought if a woman was doing these things, she couldn't possibly be holy. But Mama Antula didn't care what they thought. She only cared about being faithful to God and helping other people to know him, too.

Eventually, the people who fought against Mama Antula realized that she was right. Her work was bringing people to Jesus and helping them to know how deeply and desperately God loves every one of us. The bishop even made a rule that every seminarian had to make a retreat with Mama Antula before he could be ordained and nobody could become a priest unless she said he should. Bl. María Antonia de Paz y Figueroa preached the name of Jesus and set the hearts of Argentinean Catholics on fire, all because she knew that sometimes to be obedient to God you have to be a rebel.

Bl. María Antonia is wearing the habit of the Daughters of the Divine Savior, her bare feet visible below the hem of her tunic. In the background is the church of the Estancia de Santa Catalina, one of the Jesuit missions that was abandoned when the Jesuits were expelled. Though the Jesuits were no longer serving in Argentina, Mama Antula's work of preaching the Spiritual Exercises kept their mission alive.

Bl. María Romero Meneses

ma-REE-ah roe-MEH-roe
men-EHSS-ehss
Nicaragua, Costa Rica | 1902–1977
Feast Day: July 7

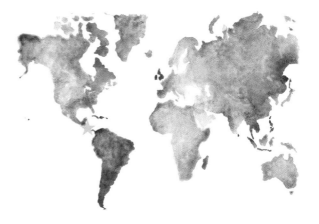

Bl. María Romero Meneses wanted to help absolutely everybody. Born into a wealthy family in Nicaragua, she was trained as an artist, a pianist, and a violinist. So when she became a Salesian Sister and was sent to Costa Rica, she was just supposed to teach wealthy girls how to draw and sing and type.

Sr. María could have become holy that way, but God was asking her to help the poor, too. That didn't mean she left the rich girls behind, though. No, she brought them with her. Her students (many of whom had never even washed a dish) went out with her to clean the homes of the poor, bring people food, and teach about Jesus.

Sr. María and her girls started small, by helping just one person, one family, one neighborhood. But the people needed more help than that. And the more Sr. María worked with them, the more big things started to fall into place. She built rec centers, where children could play and stay out of trouble. She built food banks, where hungry people could get free food. She built a school for poor girls and a clinic for sick people. And then she began building homes for poor families so they didn't have to live in dangerous neighborhoods.

Sr. María knew that it wasn't enough just to give people food and clothing. She needed to help them see that they had dignity, that it was good that they existed. She did this by helping them to build safe communities, get educated, and find good jobs, and especially by teaching them about God's love. And through all of this, Sr. María didn't take charge and work by herself. She showed people who had plenty of money that they had a responsibility to help the poor, so they worked alongside her.

Sr. María didn't just do ordinary things, however big and important. People who knew her tell of one miracle after another that was worked through her intercession. But the most amazing thing Sr. María did wasn't miraculous at all: she worked hard for nearly fifty years, helping the people of Costa Rica to rebuild their country as a more just and merciful land. In the end, everyone in Costa Rica was better off because of Bl. María Romero Meneses.

Surrounding Bl. María are medical supplies for the clinic she founded, instruments and art supplies from her classroom, canned and fresh food from her food bank, a hammer and nails from all her building projects, and one of the birds she often fed. Above her is Our Lady Help of Christians (patroness of the Salesians) who appeared to her and healed her after she was paralyzed by rheumatic fever as a child.

Bl. Maria Therese von Wüllenweber

ma-REE-ah tuh-RAY-suh fon
VOO-len-VEB-er
Germany, Italy | 1833–1907
Feast Day: December 25

Bl. Maria Therese von Wüllenweber had no idea what she was supposed to do with her life. Or, rather, she had many ideas and every one of them ended up being wrong.

Maria's dad was a baron, and she grew up in a beautiful castle in Germany, but she always felt called to be a Sister and serve the poor. After years of wondering where she might go, Maria entered the Sisters of the Sacred Heart when she was twenty-four. She thought that would be the end of her wondering, but something felt off. The Sisters were lovely, but Sr. Maria knew she needed to be serving the poor, and that wasn't really what they did.

After six years, Sr. Maria went home. It can be very discouraging to give up on a dream, but God had something else in store for her and she trusted that he would show her what it was. The very day she came home from the convent, she entered another community! This time she only stayed a few weeks, and when she came home she knew she needed to be a little more cautious before trying again. So for five years, Maria hoped and wondered. Then, at forty, she found a community that worked with the poor just the way she wanted to. It was perfect!

But two years later, Maria went back to live with her family again. She thought maybe she just needed to live out in the world and serve without entering a convent, but she couldn't find peace without a community. Finally, she met Bl. Francis Maria Jordan and the two of them began a new order together, which was just wonderful—until the other Sisters decided to change the community and split off from Sr. Maria. Once again, she was lost.

It wasn't until Maria was fifty-five years old that she founded the Salvatorian Sisters in Italy. The new community was very poor and none of them could speak Italian, but Mother Maria was finally, finally at home. All her years of wandering and wondering hadn't been wasted. God had taught her to trust him, even when she felt confused and discouraged. And it turned out that all the wandering was just what Bl. Maria Therese von Wüllenweber had needed to become holy.

Bl. Maria Therese is standing between her lay and religious lives. On the right, she's about to enjoy Kaffee und Küchen, the traditional German afternoon coffee and cake. On the table are Gugelhupf (the cake) and Westphalian quarkspeise (the cherry trifle). The painting on the wall shows her family's castle at Mönchengladbach. On the left, Mother Maria stands before the main altar at Santa Maria Maggiore, the church near the Sisters' first home in Tivoli.

St. Mariam Baouardy

MAH-ree-am bah-WAHR-dee
Palestine | 1846–1878
Feast Day: August 26

Mariam Baouardy's life was all full of suffering and all full of miracles. Her very existence was a miracle: her twelve older brothers had all died as babies, so her Melkite Catholic parents promised the Blessed Mother that if they had a healthy daughter, they would name her Mary—Mariam in Arabic. They died when she was two, so Mariam was raised by an uncle who arranged a marriage for her when she was only thirteen.

When Mariam refused, her uncle treated her terribly. She told a messenger what was happening, in the hopes that he would go for help, but all he did was tell her to become a Muslim. When she said she wouldn't, he tried to kill her! Thinking he had succeeded, he threw her body into an alley. But God had plans for Mariam, so he sent his Mother to heal her. For a month, Mary took care of Mariam, until she was nearly as good as new.

After that, Mariam began working as a maid and a cook, waiting for God to lead her to her next step. She went blind, but after forty days she was healed. She fell out a window and almost died, but got better (suddenly and completely) after a month.

Finally, Mariam went to France and tried to figure out which religious community to enter. But she was too poor for one and too sick for the next. She entered one community but was asked to leave after two years. The Sisters just weren't sure about Mariam. You see, Mariam's troubles and miracles hadn't stopped, and now she had the stigmata—the wounds of Jesus in her hands and feet and side. That was just too much for the Sisters, so they told her maybe she should go somewhere else.

In the end, Mariam entered a Carmelite convent in France. Then she helped found one in India, then ended up in Bethlehem, helping to start a Carmel in the town where Jesus was born. And all the while, she was prophesying and having visions, composing beautiful poetry even though she was simple and uneducated. After a few more years of mysticism, she had another accident, but this time there was no miracle. St. Mariam Baouardy went home to Jesus after a painful, beautiful, miraculous life.

St. Mariam is standing in the doorway of the house where she grew up, a traditional Palestinian home. She's wearing her Carmelite habit and the stigmata can be seen on her hands. The wind blowing her cloak reminds us of her powerful relationship with the Holy Spirit, who gave her miracles and visions all her life.

Bl. Marie-Clémentine Anuarite Nengapeta

ma-REE clay-mon-TEEN
AN-wah-REE-tay NENG-ah-PAY-tah
Democratic Republic of the Congo |
1939–1964
Feast Day: December 1

 Marie-Clémentine Anuarite Nengapeta wanted to belong to Jesus alone.

When Marie-Clémentine was just a little girl, her father had divorced her mother and left her and their six daughters. Marie-Clémentine forgave him. She even loved him, though she was awfully sad that he wasn't around. And she worked hard to help her mom, but all she really wanted was to be a Sister. Her mother, Julienne, did not like that idea. She wanted Marie-Clémentine to stay home and help her.

For years, Marie-Clémentine tried to convince her mother. Finally, she realized that if she was going to say yes to God's call, she would have to do it against her mother's wishes. So when she saw a truck loading up with girls who were going off to the convent, she got on that truck without telling her mother.

Now that would have been a terrible and dangerous thing to do if Marie-Clémentine had been a little girl, but she was a grown-up, and it was time for her to make her own choices. Marie-Clémentine expected her mother to make her go home again, but after a few letters Julienne gave up. Sr. Marie-Clémentine could stay!

It would have been nice if that had been the last hard thing that happened to Sr. Marie-Clémentine, but it was a very dangerous time to be a Christian in the Congo. Sr. Marie-Clémentine and her Sisters were kidnapped by the army and one of their leaders decided he wanted to marry Sr. Marie-Clémentine. She knew she would never marry him—she was already married to Jesus. She was not going to give in and she said so.

But then Olombe, one of the leader's powerful friends, tried to touch Sr. Marie-Clémentine in a way she didn't like. That is never okay, so she screamed and fought to protect herself. This made Olombe very angry, and he killed Sr. Marie-Clémentine.

But as she lay dying, she used the words that Jesus her bridegroom had said on the Cross. "I forgive you," she said. "You don't know what you're doing." And that was the most amazing thing of all. Bl. Marie-Clémentine Anuarite Nengapeta belonged to Jesus alone, in life and in death, not because she fought off her attacker but because she forgave him. That's what made her a hero and that's what will make her a Saint.

Bl. Marie-Clémentine is wearing the white habit of her order, the Sisters of the Holy Family. Behind her is the Home for Widows in Bafwabaka, the town where she entered religious life and lived as a Sister. Palm trees are found throughout the town, but the ones shown here also symbolize her martyrdom; devotional images of Sr. Marie-Clémentine generally feature palm branches quite prominently.

St. Martha Wang Luo Mande

Martha WAHNG lwoh MAHN-DEUH
(*"DEUH" like the French "de" or if you
said "wonDERful" with a British accent*)
China | 1802–1861
Feast Day: July 29

 Martha Wang Luo Mande mostly just did housework. She didn't preach or write or pray for hours and hours. She was pretty ordinary. But it turns out Jesus can do amazing things with ordinary people.

Martha and her husband were farmers and the parents of two adopted sons. But having a lovely mother doesn't always make you a lovely person, and Martha's sons were not kind. They spent all her money and when they grew up, they left their mother's house and didn't come back, even though their dad had died and their mom was all alone.

So Martha began running an inn. She hosted guests, cleaned rooms, did laundry, and cooked—especially steamed buns. She was quiet and busy, and anyone would have expected that to be the whole story of Martha Wang.

But a missionary had come to town, and Martha was amazed to hear about Jesus, who wouldn't abandon her, who would give her rest. On Christmas Day, she was baptized and given the name Martha, after a Saint who had also been hardworking and hospitable. Soon Martha moved to a town where there were more Christians, taking along a spear for the journey. "As long as there are only two or three bandits," she said, "I can spear them like soybean paste."

Martha became cook and laundress at a convent. Later she took care of children in a nursery school, loving them like they were her own. Finally, she was a cook at a seminary, feeding young men who were hoping to become priests.

People might have thought Martha was just a cook or just a cleaning lady, just a widow or just a quiet woman who never wanted much attention. But no person is unimportant and no work is unimportant. And when the government decided to ban Catholicism, Martha went to visit seminarians in prison. She brought them food and did their laundry, but she also smuggled letters in and out. And when they were finally sentenced to death, a soldier saw the quiet laundrywoman and tried to scare her by threatening to kill her, too. "Ah, well, that's fine," St. Martha Wang Luo Mande said, as simply as always. "If they can die, so can I." And the ordinary lady who nobody much noticed became a martyr and a Saint.

St. Martha is wearing simple clothes as she prepares to go visit the prison with a basket full of her famous steamed buns (and secret messages buried beneath them). She's standing beside a traditional Chinese window. Propped in the corner are the broom she used in her housework and the spear she used to protect herself on her travels.

St. Martin de Porres

mar-TEEN deh PORE-ess
(in English it's usually pronounced
MAR-tin de PORE-ez)
Peru | 1579–1639
Feast Day: November 3

People were terribly unkind to St. Martin de Porres. They made fun of him because his parents weren't married, and they made fun of him for having dark skin. They laughed because his dad was hardly ever around. That didn't change, even after Martin became a Dominican friar. Some of the friars ridiculed him because his mother had been enslaved, because his parents were different races, because they didn't like the color of his skin. Can you believe it? What a horrible thing to do, and from priests and Brothers!

But Br. Martin was really holy. So he tried his best to ignore them and to focus on his work in the sick ward and the kitchen. He was particularly useful in the kitchen, since he had a special gift with animals and knew how to ask the rodents to leave the food alone. It's true! One time, someone saw Br. Martin herding a long line of rats out into the garden; he had promised to feed them as long as they stayed out of the kitchen.

Br. Martin worked bigger miracles than that. He could be in two places at the same time—even on the other side of the planet. Once a man saw Br. Martin and thanked him again for all he had done to help enslaved people and prisoners in Africa. Another time, Br. Martin cared for a sick friend in Mexico City. The only unusual thing about all this is that Br. Martin never once left Peru.

Br. Martin had spent a few years learning how to practice medicine, and had become a good doctor. He was more than just a good doctor, actually—his healings were sometimes miraculous. But Br. Martin didn't just work miracles; he worked hard, too. He rescued orphans and built a home for them. He gave his own bed to the sick, went out into the streets to serve beggars and enslaved people, and never once refused to take care of anybody. In the end, that's what made St. Martin de Porres a Saint. It wasn't all his miracles, it was his generous heart that had never stopped loving people, no matter how cruel they had been to him. We may not be able to imitate his miracles, but we can definitely imitate his love.

St. Martin is standing in the entrance to the Convent of Santo Domingo, where he lived for many years. He's surrounded by the animals he helped in his life, including a Peruvian Inca Orchid, a breed of dog unique to Peru. We're not sure why he wore his rosary around his neck, but his earliest portrait shows him that way. That same picture shows him without the traditional black scapular and capuce worn by most lay Brothers.

St. Mary MacKillop

Australia | 1842–1909
Feast Day: August 8

 Mary MacKillop's life was not fair. Her father had a hard time making money to take care of Mary and her seven little brothers and sisters, so they were often homeless and had to be split up to live with different family members. Mary had to get a job to help; by the time she was sixteen, she was making most of the money for her family and carrying most of the stress.

When Mary's siblings were all grown, she started a religious order to teach poor children: the Sisters of St. Joseph of the Sacred Heart. Within four years nearly a hundred other women had joined! But lots of people were suspicious of the Sisters and the bishop demanded they make huge changes. Sr. Mary said that if he made these changes, she was sorry, but she couldn't belong to the order anymore. So he excommunicated her—kicked her out of the Church!

Can you believe that? But Sr. Mary knew she hadn't done anything wrong, and she trusted that God would take care of her. Within six months, the bishop realized that he had done a terrible thing, so he lifted Sr. Mary's excommunication and said the Sisters could get back to work.

After that, Sr. Mary went to the pope to get his approval of her community. But even that didn't keep priests and bishops from bothering her. Some bishops kicked the Sisters out of their dioceses. One even managed to have Sr. Mary removed as head of the order.

Do you think Sr. Mary was upset about all these things? Why, I bet she really was! But she knew God loved her, even when everything was so unfair. So she didn't complain. She just waited and prayed and trusted.

Finally, she was put in charge of the Sisters again, but before long, a stroke paralyzed her on the right side of her body. Mother Mary spent the last seven years of her life in a wheelchair, learning to write with her left hand so she could continue to serve the Sisters as they served the poor. Not one bit of it was fair—but that didn't matter. St. Mary MacKillop was loved. She was faithful. And in the end, her life was a great gift to the Church in Australia and eventually to the world.

St. Mary is wearing the habit of the Sisters of St. Joseph of the Sacred Heart; because the habit is brown, the Sisters are called "Brown Joeys" after St. Joseph (and a nod to baby kangaroos). The blue braid on her habit is an interlocking A and M for "Ave Maria" or "auspice Maria" (meaning "under the protection of Mary"). Later in life, Mother Mary had an Australian Terrier named Bobs, who appears in this picture with her.

St. Monica

Algeria, Italy | 331–387
Feast Day: August 27

St. Monica prayed and prayed and prayed for her son. For fifteen years, nothing happened. But she just kept praying.

Monica was used to unanswered prayers. She had prayed for her husband Patricius for years, too, begging God to convert his heart. Patricius wasn't kind to Monica and he wasn't a Christian. No matter how hard Monica prayed and no matter how kind and gentle she was, that just didn't change—until the very end of Patricius' life. Just before his death, Patricius was baptized.

Monica was delighted! But by then, she had another big prayer intention: her son, who we now call St. Augustine, was not at all saintly. He was sixteen years old and he was a mess. He didn't love God and he didn't make good choices. Pretty soon, he moved to a new city and Monica could only write him letters telling him she was worried sick. Monica was pretty sure that wouldn't do much good, but she knew that prayer works. So she just kept praying.

The trouble was that Augustine had to choose God. No matter how hard Monica prayed, God wouldn't *make* Augustine love him. Monica didn't give up, but she wasn't always happy about how long she had to wait. All her sorrow over Augustine's sins and all her worrying that he would never repent meant she spent a lot of time crying.

When Augustine moved to Milan, so did Monica, and she kept praying and weeping. Then, *finally*, all her prayers were answered. Augustine had heard about God for years and years, but now he came to know and love God at last. He realized, quite suddenly, that everything his mother had been preaching was true. Soon, Augustine was baptized by St. Ambrose, and Monica was rewarded for her years of prayer.

And it's a good thing Augustine was converted when he was. Monica died a few months later. She never saw her son ordained a priest or a bishop. She had no idea that he would become one of the most important theologians of all time. But she knew he was a lover of Jesus, and that was a dream come true for her. And now the Church has one of her greatest Saints because his mother St. Monica never stopped praying.

St. Monica was probably an Amazigh (Berber) woman. We chose to depict her with the clothes and accessories of the Kabyle people, including their traditional striped pattern. She's holding a Kabyle water jug and standing by the pear tree that Augustine wrote about in his Confessions. *The grapevines in the background remind us of Monica's habit of drinking too much wine in her youth.*

St. Moses the Strong

Egypt, Ethiopia | 330–405
Feast Day: August 28

St. Moses the Strong had made some very, very bad choices. He was the leader of a band of outlaws who stole and killed and roamed all around terrifying people. Moses got angrier and scarier as the years went by. Once, he was so mad that a dog had barked at him that he swam across the whole Nile River with a knife between his teeth so that he could attack the dog's owner!

Eventually, Moses found himself on the run from the law. He decided to hide in a monastery way out in the Egyptian desert, but once he was there he began to wonder at the gentleness and kindness and mercy the monks showed him. Overcome by the love of Jesus, Moses soon asked to be a monk, too.

Can you imagine? The biggest, toughest, most dangerous man in all of Egypt was giving up his life of crime to live for Jesus? It was a miracle! But conversion isn't usually easy, and Moses had a lot of converting to do. He had to learn to control his temper and all his other passions, and that was going to take time.

Once, some outlaws came to rob the monastery, not knowing that the man who had once terrified them was there. Before they knew it, Moses had tied them all up, and carried them into the chapel.

"Um . . . it used to be I would have killed them," he said. "But I think we don't do that?"

"Let them go free," the Brothers said. Moses was amazed—he had never seen mercy like that. Neither had the thieves. They were so shocked, they decided to stay and be monks, too!

Moses was discouraged by how slowly he became holy, but he kept at it. And gradually, he was freed from his old vices and filled with wisdom and mercy instead. He was ordained a priest and then made abbot. When his monks heard that some men were coming to kill them, they wanted to fight to protect their abbey. Moses told them to run away. But, remembering how much he had been forgiven, St. Moses the Strong stayed. He welcomed the murderers with open arms and was killed, no longer vicious and vengeful, but a man of mercy with a martyr's crown.

St. Moses is standing outside the entrance to the Paromeos Monastery in Wadi El Natrun. A story is told that Abba Moses was called in to judge another monk and came with a skin filled with water (or sand) leaking behind him. "My sins run out behind me," he said, "and I do not see them, but today I am coming to judge the errors of another." The Brothers took his correction and forgave the wayward monk.

Bl. Nicholas Bunkerd Kitbamrung

Nicholas BOOHN-kurd kit-BAHM-rung
(BOOHN is like book, but with an n)
Thailand | 1895–1944
Feast Day: January 12

Bl. Nicholas Bunkerd Kitbamrung was awfully stubborn. His teachers noticed it a few years before he was supposed to be ordained, and they were worried. A man like that wouldn't make a very good priest. He was arrogant and selfish. What good would he be to his people?

But God was working on Nicholas, and he began to change. His stubbornness didn't go away—that's not usually how grace works. Instead, it was transformed into persistence. Instead of insisting on having his own way, whatever other people thought, he became focused and committed. It was the same instinct, the same personality, but purified.

It's a good thing Nicholas had the gift of perseverance—he had to spend eighteen years in the seminary! And when he was finally ordained, he had a lot of work to do. He traveled around Thailand trying to convince Catholics who had stopped going to Mass to come back. He taught other priests Thai while he was learning a Chinese dialect, all because he wanted as many people as possible to come to know Jesus. Fr. Nicholas's stubbornness was beginning to pay off, now that it was given over to Jesus.

People in Thailand were suspicious of Catholics at that time, and Fr. Nicholas knew it. He knew they wanted him to stop preaching the Gospel, and he didn't care. He wasn't going to give up the work God had given him to do. Not even when he was arrested for ringing church bells. It was a silly charge, but the government had decided that Fr. Nicholas was a spy, so they sent him to prison for fifteen years.

But persistent Fr. Nicholas thought prison was the perfect place to work for the Lord. In the three years that he spent in prison before dying of tuberculosis, Fr. Nicholas baptized sixty-eight people. He preached to the prisoners and prayed with them and brought dozens of them to Jesus, all because he refused to give up. Fr. Nicholas had been stubborn, but when he gave his life to the Lord, God had helped him come alive. He hadn't changed completely, he'd just been purified. And so, fully himself but fully Christ's, Bl. Nicholas Bunkerd Kitbamrung won a martyr's crown.

Bl. Nicholas is standing in his prison cell with a small bowl of water, ready to baptize one of the prisoners. The book in his hand indicates that he continued to preach and teach in prison. His uniform is modeled on a mural from his shrine in Thailand, and his stance and facial expression show his determination to continue serving the Lord.

Bl. Nicolas Steno

Nicolas STEH-no
Denmark, Germany | 1638–1686
Feast Day: December 5

Did you know that you can be a scientist and a Saint? You can even study fossils and dinosaur bones and be a Saint—Bl. Nicolas Steno is proof.

Nicolas Steno was a genius. He figured out how muscles work and he figured out how blood moves in our bodies and he figured out where spit comes from and he figured out that fossils come from plants and animals that died a long, long time ago. But the most important thing he figured out was about the layers of the earth's crust and how they form. His research is the reason we can tell now which dinosaurs lived at which time. It led to the science of paleontology and it got him named "the father of geology."

But amazing discoveries don't make you a Saint and at this point in his life, Nicolas wasn't even a Catholic. He was Protestant, so he was a Christian who believed in Jesus but didn't believe in the Eucharist or follow the pope. But the more Nicolas studied, the more he realized that the Catholic Church was true. And finally, one day, he saw a Eucharistic procession, where hundreds of people were kneeling before Jesus in the Blessed Sacrament, and he knew he had to make a choice. Either this was really Jesus or it was a lie.

Nicolas knew that Jesus had said, "This is my body," so he decided it must be true.

He became Catholic. After that, he kept working as a scientist. He believed that learning about the world God made was a way of praising God.

After a few years, though, he realized God was calling him to be a priest—and, only two years later, a bishop! His job was to try to bring Protestant Christians home to the Catholic Church, and he put his whole heart into it, just as he put his whole heart into science. So he left behind a job that impressed everybody, and went instead to fast and pray and speak about the Church to people who wanted nothing to do with it. Bl. Nicolas Steno was very poor and very wise and his life brought many people to God, which is even more important than all the most amazing scientific discoveries in the world.

Bl. Nicolas is wearing the bishop's garb featured in one of his earliest portraits. He holds one of the rocks that he studied; in the other hand, he holds a monstrance like the one that brought about his conversion. All around him are his scientific diagrams and the frontispieces of his books on theology as well as science. The top right features human organs interspersed with flowers; the bottom right shows his hypothesized source of fossilized teeth.

St. Nina of Georgia

NEE-na of Georgia
Georgia | 296–340
Feast Day: January 14

St. Nina of Georgia was just a slave girl. That's what everybody thought, anyway. Actually, that's what Nina thought. She had been captured and taken to the country of Georgia, where nobody was Christian. Some people would have given up on Jesus then—either because there were no priests and nobody to pray with or because being enslaved is a miserable, awful thing and sometimes it's hard to love God when life is miserable and awful.

But Nina kept praying and loving and trying to trust that God was working even in her tragedy. Still, she knew that she was just a slave girl. What could God possibly do through her?

Apparently Nina had forgotten about the great good God had done through a poor village girl in Nazareth. She had forgotten that God can do miracles through anybody at all, however small and unimportant. And she had forgotten that God is always, always, always working in our lives, even when it seems like he's not there.

Still, Nina kept praying. She prayed so much that people began to ask her about it. So Nina told them about Jesus, about how Jesus healed the sick and raised the dead and loved the weak and saved us all. And because she was so holy, they kept asking. And listening. And learning to love Jesus.

Once, Nina's prayers healed a dying child. After that, the queen of Georgia, who had been sick for a long time, wanted to meet Nina. Nina didn't think that made any sense. She was just a slave. What could the queen possibly want from her?

And would you believe it? That's the message Nina sent back. To the queen! She was so convinced that she wasn't worth much, Nina refused to go. So the queen went to Nina, who prayed for her and saw a miracle happen: the queen was healed.

After that, the queen wanted to become Christian, which meant a lot of people wanted to become Christians. The king refused at first, but then he had a miracle of his own and converted, and the whole country along with him. St. Nina of Georgia had thought she was just a slave girl, but she became the apostle to a whole nation, all because she believed in God even when she didn't believe in herself.

St. Nina is pausing to contemplate a cross made of grapevine. Legend has it that the Blessed Mother herself told Nina to preach the Gospel in Georgia. Mary gave Nina a grapevine cross to give her strength, which Nina then twined her own hair into to secure it. The cross is kept to this day in the Orthodox cathedral in Tbilisi, and a cross with drooping arms has become the symbol of the Church in Georgia.

St. Olga of Kiev

OLE-gah of Kiev
Russia, Ukraine | d. 969
Feast Day: July 11

 Olga of Kiev got what she deserved. Olga was a queen, but not the tea-parties-and-lapdogs kind. Olga was more the vicious-and-violent kind. So when her husband was killed, Olga decided to get her revenge—and a ferocious reputation. Her son was king now, but he was only two years old. And if Olga was going to rule in his place, she had to be terrifying. And teach her son to be terrifying. Soon, Olga was a powerful, brilliant, successful queen. Everything was going perfectly.

But then something happened that Queen Olga hadn't planned on. While visiting Constantinople, Olga decided to be baptized.

We're not exactly sure that Olga got baptized for the right reasons. Since most of the other rulers were Christians, she may just have been trying to get more power. But either way, her baptism worked. Olga was changed. She began to pray, to fast, to serve the poor. This violent woman (who had killed thousands of people) suddenly wanted to be holy.

When Olga was baptized, all her guilt was taken away (and there was a lot of guilt). But Olga had made some choices that even baptism couldn't reverse. The people she'd had killed were still dead. Her son the king was cruel and violent, just as his mother had hoped, and nothing she said or did could change that. She told him all about Jesus' love, but he just rolled his eyes at his poor, changed mother.

Olga went out to tell the people about Jesus, but they weren't interested. For fifteen years, Olga got what she deserved. She had been wicked, and now everybody she loved was wicked, too, and there was nothing she could do about it.

Olga didn't give up. She kept praying and talking about God. She kept inviting missionaries to her country. None of it worked. When Olga died, her people were as pagan as ever.

But Olga's grandson had watched her pray and preach and love her people. And he couldn't resist the power of her prayers from heaven. Finally, years after Olga's death, St. Vladimir was baptized. After that, nearly the whole country became Christian! St. Olga of Kiev had gotten what she deserved in her life, but in death she received only mercy: the kingdom of heaven and a Christian kingdom on earth, besides.

St. Olga is standing with her grandson St. Vladimir, who's holding the bright yellow Orthodox Cathedral of St. Vladimir in Kiev. This shows that he was the founder of the Church in the country (through the witness and intercession of his grandmother). She's holding a cross over her head to announce the Gospel to her people and is dressed in fur-lined royal clothes to keep warm.

St. Oscar Romero

OSS-cur roe-MARE-oh
El Salvador | 1917–1980
Feast Day: March 24

St. Oscar Romero wasn't afraid anymore.

He had always been nervous and shy. When he was a young priest and even a young bishop, he had ignored the evil that was being done in El Salvador. He just celebrated Mass and heard Confessions and left the rest alone. That was why the wicked men in the government wanted him to be archbishop of San Salvador—they knew he wouldn't cause them any trouble. He was too scared and too weak to do what he knew was right.

Then the government killed his friend Venerable Rutilio Grande, a priest who was helping the poor, and something inside Archbishop Romero changed. He knew that being quiet wasn't protecting anybody but him. He had abandoned the poor and the weak. "If I don't change now," he said to himself, "I never will." So Archbishop Romero began to be brave. He preached against the evil that was being done to the people. He listened to them and spent time with them.

He was making dangerous people very angry. But Archbishop Romero had become so brave that he wasn't worried about his life anymore. He knew the government would kill him. He didn't care. He had one life, and he wanted to use it to help his scared, starving, broken people.

So Archbishop Romero stood up during Mass and preached a homily begging soldiers not to follow unjust orders: "I ask you, I beg you, I command you in the name of God: stop the oppression!"

He was right, of course—nobody can be ordered to do something evil. But he was also encouraging soldiers to fight back against the officers who led them. And he knew that sooner or later, that homily would cost him his life.

It only took one day for them to come for him. Archbishop Romero was celebrating Mass, preaching that people mustn't love themselves so much that they refuse to take risks for others. After his homily, a shot rang out and he fell to the ground, killed while celebrating Mass. St. Oscar Romero had decided to start living from love instead of living from fear. It had cost him his life, but won him a martyr's crown and the love of a people who knew how much he loved them.

St. Oscar is standing in front of his cathedral in San Salvador, the Cathedral of the Holy Savior. The cross in the background is a large cross in Concepcion de Ataco; though it can't be seen from San Salvador, it's often depicted in artwork of the city. The little houses in the background symbolize the homes of the poor people he served.

Bl. Paul Thoj Xyooj

Paul tao SHIONG
Laos | 1941–1960
Feast Day: December 16

Bl. Paul Thoj Xyooj was a huge success! And then he was a big failure. But he was never a quitter. Nobody in his village had ever heard of Jesus until missionaries came when Xyooj (Shiong) was nine. For years he listened to the missionaries' preaching and when he was sixteen he went off to study for the priesthood.

A year later, he was home again. Xyooj had discerned that God wasn't calling him to be a priest. This was no failure—it had been a triumph to go to seminary and now it was a triumph to come home, though it didn't always feel that way. God's will is always the best place to be, even when it looks a little like failure.

Since none of the priests spoke Hmong, Xyooj went with them as a missionary to another Hmong village. But Xyooj was so handsome and his clothes were so regal, the villagers thought he must be a king. "I am no king," Xyooj said, "but have come to tell you of Jesus, the king who vanquishes all demons." The people were amazed! They were very afraid of evil spirits, and here was a God who could conquer them all.

So Xyooj taught and they listened. They couldn't get enough. By the third day, half the people in the village wanted to be baptized. Xyooj was a great success! Like the Hmong shamans, he rang a gong to gather the people. Unlike the shamans, he was there to talk about Jesus, and hundreds of people came.

But the priests in charge of Laos were suspicious. They thought maybe Xyooj wasn't preaching the whole Gospel and that's why people were excited. So they made Xyooj leave the people he loved. He was awfully hurt, but he obeyed. Then for almost six months he waited and wondered, feeling abandoned.

But he didn't give up on the Church, even when it seemed like the Church had given up on him. Before long, he was sent on another mission. But he and Bl. Mario Borzaga, the priest he was with, didn't realize what danger they were in. They were ambushed and killed by communist soldiers. Bl. Paul Thoj Xyooj had been a success and a failure but in the end he was totally Christ's, which is really all that matters.

Bl. Xyooj is wearing traditional Hmong dress, including three large silver collars given him by his father. It was these collars that convinced the people that he was a young man of importance. He's holding a picture of the Sacred Heart like the one he used to teach the people about Jesus; a similar image was found in the backpack of Bl. Mario Borzaga when he was captured. In the tree is a green peacock, which is found throughout Laos.

St. Pedro de San José Betancur

PEH-dro deh SAN hoe-ZAY
beh-tahn-COOR
Spain (Canary Islands), Guatemala |
1626–1667
Feast Day: April 25

 St. Pedro de San José Betancur didn't have a selfish bone in his body.

Pedro grew up poor, watching his family's small flock of sheep. But when he was twelve he had to become an indentured servant, which is only a little better than a slave. For eleven years, he had lots of work to do and no freedom at all.

You would think that the moment he was set free, Pedro would have eaten a huge meal, taken a long nap, and made plans for a comfortable life. But Pedro had heard about how people all the way across the world were suffering (especially Indigenous and Black people) so he left his home off the coast of Africa and set sail for the Americas. When he got to Cuba, he had to work to earn money so he could keep going. Even then Pedro only had enough to get to Honduras, so he walked the rest of the way to Guatemala. When he finally got there, he was so poor he had to go to a soup kitchen for food just like the people he was trying to help.

But Pedro wasn't sorry. He was just excited to be in the country where he was going to serve! He tried to become a Jesuit priest, but he wasn't educated enough; after three years they asked him to leave. That's when Pedro gave up on plans and just started to serve. He walked around the nicest parts of town ringing a bell to ask for donations and inviting the rich to love Jesus better. He brought the Advent tradition of Las Posadas to Guatemala. He visited prisons and hospitals, taught people to read, worked with lepers and the elderly, served the poor and enslaved, and always reminded the people around him that *everyone* has dignity. Everyone deserves love. Everyone deserves respect.

Eventually, Pedro had inspired so many people to join him in his work that his followers became the first new religious order of the Americas: the Bethlehemites. These men worked with Br. Pedro, in the hospital that he'd built, the homeless shelter that he'd opened, and the school that he'd founded. But Br. Pedro never cared much about buildings and programs. All his life, all St. Pedro de San José Betancur wanted was to love people, whatever the cost.

St. Pedro is holding the tambourine he played during the Christmas season. He carried a hat under his arm with holy cards of baby Jesus inside it; he never wore the hat, saying he was always in the presence of God. His clothes are modeled on a portrait painted during his lifetime. In the background is the volcano Pacaya, which erupted three times while Pedro lived nearby.

Sts. Perpetua & Felicity

Tunisia | 183–203
Feast Day: March 7

 Perpetua's heart was broken. She didn't so much mind being in prison and she wasn't at all afraid to die. She just missed her baby. He was so little and he needed her. But Perpetua was going to be martyred. The only way out of it was to deny Jesus, and she knew she could never do that. So she was going to have to say goodbye to her baby. Forever.

St. Felicity hadn't had her baby yet. But she knew that just as soon as she did, she would have to give the baby to another mother to raise. She would kiss her baby goodbye and go off to be killed for her faith.

But Perpetua and Felicity had each other. They had other Christians, there in the prison with them. And they had the Holy Spirit. Things had been harder before they had been baptized. But now what joy there was to know they'd been set free from their sin!

Still, you can find joy in Jesus and be dreadfully sad at the same time. Perpetua was miserable because she missed her baby and worried about what would happen to him. Felicity was anxious that she wouldn't be killed with her friends, since she was still pregnant. What would happen if she had to be martyred all by herself?

So Perpetua prayed to hold her baby one last time and Felicity prayed to have her baby in time. Both prayers were answered. Perpetua held and nursed and loved her little boy until it was time to entrust him to a new mother. And after Felicity's baby girl was born right there in the prison, Felicity's sister took her home and became her mother.

After this, Perpetua and Felicity's broken hearts began to mend. They knew that God would take care of their children. They knew that from heaven, they would be able to pray for their little ones. And they knew that the time was coming to give their lives for the God who gave his life for them. So they fixed their hair, straightened their clothes, and smiled as they walked singing to their deaths. Sts. Perpetua and Felicity were killed in the arena, their broken hearts healed as they went home to Jesus.

St. Perpetua is snuggling her baby while St. Felicity is waiting for her baby's birth. Their clothes, coloring, and carefully styled hair are modeled on the Fayum mummy portraits, first- to third-century images from Roman Egypt. The pitcher represents their baptism while in prison and Perpetua's statement to her father that as a pitcher could be called by no other name, she could be called by no name but Christian.

Bl. Peter Donders

Peter DOHN-dehrss
Netherlands, Suriname | 1809–1887
Feast Day: January 14

Nobody wanted Bl. Peter Donders. The Redemptorists didn't want him. The Jesuits didn't want him. The Franciscans didn't want him. He was poor and he was sickly and he wasn't very clever and nobody thought he would be much use.

But Peter knew God was calling him, so he kept trying. Finally, he convinced a bishop to ordain him and send him to Suriname, a Dutch-speaking country in South America. Peter had dreamed of working in the foreign missions, bringing the hope of Jesus to people who had never heard of him, and finally he was on his way. It didn't matter that nobody had wanted him, that he had done so poorly in school, that he had been a shy and awkward man in classes with little boys who had teased and bullied him. Fr. Peter had persevered, and now he was a priest.

Maybe all that struggle—of being teased and ignored and rejected—was what made Fr. Peter such a gift to the people of Suriname. When he got there, he found thousands and thousands of people who were far more despised than he had been. There were many enslaved people, who were treated worse than animals, and Indigenous people who were treated almost as badly. And then there were the lepers, who had a terrible, painful disease and were sent away to live and die ignored by the people who should have loved them.

Fr. Peter served them all. He preached to them and loved them and fought for them, begging the government to take better care of these abused people. Fighting against slavery was considered treason, so Fr. Peter served enslaved people instead. He served Indigenous people, spending hours and hours on a riverboat to get to villages in the jungle where he could tell the people about Jesus. And he served the sick, spending thirty years in a leper colony loving the people the world had forgotten.

By the time Bl. Peter Donders died (when he was almost eighty) he had spent nearly forty-five years loving people who were abused and unloved by the world. The young man nobody wanted had given his life to love hurting and oppressed people—all because he knew God loved them (and him) with an everlasting love. No matter what.

Bl. Peter is wearing his Redemptorist habit as he takes a riverboat to a Maroon village. The Maroon people were descended from Black people who escaped slavery and fled into the wilderness to live. Though Fr. Peter mostly worked with Indigenous people and people with leprosy, he tried to evangelize Maroon people as well. Only a few of the Maroons converted (as opposed to hundreds of Indigenous people each year), but he continued to visit.

Bl. Peter Kasui Kibe

Peter KAH-soo-ee KEE-beh
Japan | 1587–1639
Feast Day: July 1

Bl. Peter Kasui Kibe never, never, never gave up.

Born into a Christian samurai family, Kibe knew God was calling him to be a Jesuit priest. But when he asked to join, they told him they didn't think he was committed enough. Kibe volunteered with them for eight years, but before they changed their minds, the missionaries got kicked out of the country. Kibe went with them to China, but the seminary there told him he couldn't be a priest because he was Japanese. He went on to India, but they told him they wouldn't ordain anyone Asian at all.

Now is that okay? Of course it isn't! It's never okay to reject people or be cruel to them because of how they look or where their ancestors came from. Kibe could have decided to give up on being a priest after traveling so far and being refused again and again. But God was calling him, and he would follow. He decided he would ask in Rome—and that he would walk there. He walked nearly four thousand miles, and when he finally got to Rome he found people who didn't just look at him, they listened. Within six months, he was a priest.

After that, everyone warned him that Japanese Christians were being killed in brutal ways. They said he should stay in Europe, but Fr. Kibe knew his people needed him. So off he sailed, to Goa and then China and then Thailand and the Philippines. Nobody would help him get to Japan. He was chased by pirates. He was shipwrecked on a boat he built himself. He didn't quit.

Finally—*finally*—Fr. Kibe got to Japan. It had taken him eight years to get there from Europe. It had taken him twenty-four years from when he first asked to be a Jesuit priest until he finally arrived back home as a Jesuit priest. All the while he knew he was on his way to torture and certain death, but he never gave up. For nine years he lived in hiding in Japan, bringing people the sacraments until he was betrayed and arrested. But no matter how they tortured him, Fr. Kibe never gave up his faith. In the end, his captors killed him: Bl. Peter Kasui Kibe, the most determined man on the face of the planet.

Bl. Kibe is standing on the shore, having finally reached Japan in the tiny fishing boat behind him. Mount Fuji is in the background, as is a large wave reminiscent of the famous print "The Great Wave off Kanagawa" by Japanese artist Hokusai. To avoid detection, Fr. Kibe is wearing the clothes of a Japanese layman instead of his Jesuit cassock.

Bl. Peter To Rot

Peter TOE ROTE
Papua New Guinea | 1912–1945
Feast Day: July 7

Bl. Peter To Rot really just wanted an ordinary life.

To Rot (whose name rhymes with "row boat") grew up in a Catholic family, the son of the village chief. He was sent away to school to learn how to teach the faith to others. When he came home again, he told everyone about Jesus, his Bible always in his hand. To Rot got married, and he and his wife prayed together every morning and every evening. It was a lovely, ordinary life.

But soon, Papua New Guinea was invaded by the Japanese army. The soldiers who came to To Rot's village arrested all the missionaries, which left To Rot in charge. Suddenly, he had a very important and very dangerous job. He couldn't celebrate Mass, but he could bring people Communion, baptize people, and even witness marriages. He could take people to a priest who was hiding in the forest, and he could lead them in prayer every Sunday. And when the Japanese soldiers destroyed the church, To Rot went into the woods and built a secret chapel out of tree branches.

The soldiers were worried that the people were praying against them. They wanted to get between the people and God. So when they couldn't get To Rot to stop leading Christians in prayer, they decided to lead them into sin by saying that men should have more than one wife.

To Rot knew this was wrong. He told the men not to hurt God and their wives this way. He even stopped a wicked Catholic man from kidnapping a woman to force her into marriage. When the man tried again, To Rot rescued the woman and took her to safety.

It was all too much. On Christmas Day, To Rot was in his garden picking vegetables to offer as a gift to his enemies when they came to his home and dragged him to prison. His wife, who was pregnant with their third child, begged him to promise that he would stop talking about Jesus, but To Rot couldn't do that. He knew they would kill him for it, but he had to do what was right—even though it would cost him his life. Bl. Peter To Rot had wanted an ordinary life, but all the ordinary things built him up into an extraordinary man and a martyr.

Bl. To Rot is standing in the doorway of a small hut, similar to the chapel he secretly built in the forest to serve his people. On the bottom he's wearing a traditional Tolai waistcloth, on the top a western button down shirt. He's holding the Bible and cross he used as a catechist. The Raggiana bird-of-paradise pictured is the national bird of Papua New Guinea; its feathers are often used in traditional dress and art.

St. Peter Wu Guosheng

Peter WOO gwoh-SHENG
China | 1768–1814
Feast Day: November 7

St. Peter Wu Guosheng was not a quiet man. He was the kind of guy who shouts with delight when you walk into a room and drags you over to meet all his friends. He was loud and effusive and very excited about quite a lot of things.

So when Guosheng was working at the hotel he and his wife owned and he met a missionary for the first time, he wanted to know just absolutely everything about Jesus. And when he heard how God made the world for love of us and became a man to save us from our sin, Guosheng thought this was just the most amazing thing! He began to grab people off the street, dragging them into the hotel to sit down and hear all about the Gospel.

It was lovely. But it was also very dangerous. Christians were being persecuted in China and Guosheng needed to learn to be a little more careful. Besides, Fr. Luo, the missionary, wasn't sure about this man who was so excited so quickly. Would he get bored with the faith and move on after he had been baptized? Fr. Luo decided Guosheng needed to wait a while before he could become Catholic.

Guosheng had always been loud and passionate and outgoing. And it was good that he was that way—God had made him that way and he loved Guosheng exactly as he was. But Guosheng began to realize that he needed to be a little more cautious, a little gentler. He learned when to shout and when to speak more calmly, when to talk on and on and on and when to listen.

Pretty soon, he was ready to be baptized. After that, Guosheng was a force, but not an overwhelming one anymore. He preached the Gospel and turned his hotel into a Christian community and led almost six hundred people to Jesus. Eventually, the authorities caught up with him, but even in prison Guosheng's voice could be heard, leading the others in prayer and preaching the Gospel to those who didn't know Jesus yet. St. Peter Wu Guosheng became the first native Chinese martyr, not by running from his big personality but by handing himself over to Jesus to be big and loud (and sometimes gentle and quiet) for Jesus.

St. Guosheng is standing in the door of a nineteenth-century Chinese inn, his hands held in a traditional Chinese greeting. His face shows a big smile and a mouth wide open, ready to call out to people and tell them about Jesus. A rosary is shown hanging from his side because he prayed the Rosary in prison and on the way to his death.

Bl. Pier Giorgio Frassati

pyehr JORE-joe frah-SAH-tee
Italy | 1901–1925
Feast Day: July 4

Some people think Saints shouldn't be silly. They think Saints shouldn't play jokes or go to parties or ski or climb mountains or go to the theater.

If you had told Bl. Pier Giorgio Frassati that, he would have laughed and laughed.

Pier Giorgio did a lot of laughing. He also did a lot of horseback riding and loud (off-key) singing. His friends called him "an explosion of joy." He wasn't a very good student, but he was a very, very good friend—to the other young people in Turin and to the poor and sick and lonely. You see, Pier Giorgio loved to have fun especially as a way of helping people to feel the joy of Jesus. So he had fun when he went hiking with his friends and when he brought food to the hungry. He laughed with the kids in his class and with sick old ladies. His motto was "to the heights"—to the top of the mountains he was climbing and to the heights of holiness.

You would think his parents would have been awfully proud of their kind, generous, holy son. But they weren't. Pier Giorgio's parents didn't know Jesus, and they didn't want him to spend so much time in prayer. They were fancy and clever and important and they wished he would spend more time getting ahead and less time getting to church.

Pier Giorgio's parents didn't like each other very much, and the more frustrated they became with Pier Giorgio, the more frustrated they became with each other. So Pier Giorgio tried awfully hard not to upset them. He didn't tell them when he went to Mass very early in the morning, even when he gave his bus fare to the poor and had to run home. He didn't tell them about the ways he helped suffering people, even when he stayed home from vacations with his friends because he didn't want to leave the poor without help.

Bl. Pier Giorgio Frassati was out taking care of the sick when he caught the disease that would kill him. But even this was no tragedy to the laughing saint—he knew heaven would be much more fun than earth had been, and he was ready to go to the heights in death as he had in life.

Bl. Pier Giorgio is shown in his favorite place: the mountains. He's climbing "verso l'alto" ("to the heights!") on one of his many hiking excursions through the Italian Alps; in the background is the Matterhorn, which he had planned to climb in celebration of his college graduation.

St. Pulcheria

pool-KEHR-ee-ah
Turkey | 399–453
Feast Day: September 10

St. Pulcheria was the most powerful woman in the world. Her father had been the Byzantine emperor, but he died when Pulcheria was only nine. This left Pulcheria's seven-year-old brother Theodosius to be emperor, though he had grown-ups to make all the decisions for him. Pulcheria decided that she would be in charge of Theodosius' education. And then, when she was fifteen, she told her brother's advisors that they weren't needed anymore—Pulcheria could run the empire, thank you very much.

At only fifteen—can you imagine? Pulcheria ruled for her brother, and then when he was old enough they ruled together. And in between all the necessary meetings and banquets, Pulcheria was praying. She and her sisters became consecrated virgins, married to Jesus, and would spend hours in prayer. But when duty called, Pulcheria would leave her spot in the chapel to go rule the empire, balancing her life of prayer with her very important work.

Eventually, Theodosius decided he didn't need Pulcheria anymore, so he sent her away. Pulcheria was only too happy to leave the palace and have all the time she wanted for prayer. But with his sister gone, Theodosius was lost. He didn't really understand what was going on in the empire and he *really* didn't understand what was going on in the Church. Before long, he had gotten all confused and Pulcheria had to come back to court to help him again.

She stayed there as empress for the rest of her life. When Theodosius died, Pulcheria ruled by herself, and then (when the empire was fighting off Attila the Hun) with a general named Marcian as emperor beside her. She was so wise and so holy that when all the bishops of the Church were having trouble figuring out what it meant that Jesus was God, Pope St. Leo the Great asked Pulcheria to come speak to the Council of Chalcedon and explain who Jesus is: fully God and fully man, one person with two natures. And when she died, Pulcheria left her whole fortune to the poor, to build hospitals and churches for them.

St. Pulcheria isn't a Saint because she was brilliant and powerful and rich. She's a Saint because she was Christ's, because she was humble and obedient, because everything she did was for Jesus. That's real power.

St. Pulcheria's headdress (with strings of pearls) and decorative collar are modeled on a sixth-century sculpture of the Empress Ariadne. Her clothes are modeled on a sixth-century mosaic of Empress Theodora in Ravenna. On the left is the Church of the Holy Apostles, first built in the fourth century. On the right (overlooking the Sea of Marmara) is the Boukoleon Palace, which was built during Pulcheria's reign.

St. Rafael Guízar y Valencia

rahf-ah-YEL GHEE-sar ee
bah-LEN-see-ah
Mexico | 1878–1938
Feast Day: June 6

Would you think that playing the accordion could save your life? Or that dressing up in disguises could save souls? St. Rafael Guízar y Valencia probably didn't think so—at first. How could he know that his Catholic country would become such a dangerous place to be a priest?

But before Fr. Rafael had been ordained for ten years, an awful war began in Mexico and the government started killing priests. Fr. Rafael decided to hide in plain sight, dressing up as a junk dealer, a doctor, and a musician and bringing people the sacraments. Once, he was arrested for being a priest. He insisted he was a musician, but they didn't believe him. "Can I at least have something to eat?" he asked, then gobbled down four sandwiches in a row!

"Why are you *so hungry*?" his captors asked.

"I had to sell my instrument, so I can't make money for food," Fr. Rafael explained.

Suspicious, they brought him an accordion. When Fr. Rafael (who really was a musician) began to play beautifully, they apologized and let him go—with the accordion and fifty pesos. Tricky Fr. Rafael was free again!

But there was only so long Fr. Rafael could sneak around. Eventually he fled to Texas, Guatemala, then Cuba; everywhere he went he worked to serve the poor. But after a few years of exile, Fr. Rafael was named bishop in Mexico. So back he went, despite the danger.

Soon, the governor told the people that anyone who killed Bishop Rafael would get a lot of money for doing it. Bishop Rafael could have gone into hiding, but his people needed him. So he marched right across town and into the governor's office. Then he looked that wicked man in the eye and said, "If you want me dead, you kill me yourself. I will *not* have you tempting my people to sin just so they can feed their families." The governor had never seen someone so brave! He was so impressed (and maybe so intimidated) that he decided to let the bishop go free.

St. Rafael Guízar y Valencia spent the rest of his life serving in freedom, with no disguises. But he was always grateful for the dress-up clothes and the accordion that had helped him be an undercover priest all those years earlier.

St. Rafael is wearing a sombrero to keep off the hot sun as he rides his mule around southeastern Mexico. He often traveled with the army so he could serve the wounded, and occasionally he came home with bullet holes in his hat. Fr. Rafael is disguised in a shirt and tie here with an accordion on his back so that the police would take him for a musician.

St. Rafqa Pietra Choboq Ar-Rayès

RAHFF-kah PYEH-trah
SHOOH-booh ar RIE-ess
Lebanon | 1832–1914
Feast Day: March 23

When most people are terribly, terribly sick, they pray for God to heal them. Not St. Rafqa Pietra Choboq Ar-Rayès. She was happy to suffer. Rafqa had discovered that in her pain, she was able to come closer to Jesus than she ever did when she was well. She was able to offer him her suffering, which only helped her love him more.

And Rafqa suffered a lot. Her mom died when she was little and she had to go live with another family for years. Then when she was grown, her family fought bitterly over who she would marry, when Rafqa just wanted to be a nun. After she entered the convent, she lived through a terrifying time when wicked men killed lots and lots of people. Then her religious order shut down and Rafqa was lost again. Finally, she became a Maronite nun and was so happy to be home at last.

But Sr. Rafqa started getting dreadful headaches and even worse eye aches. She smiled through it all, but her superior made her go to a doctor. And when the doctor was performing the surgery, he accidentally cut her right eye out! Then she went blind in her left eye, too. But would you believe it? All the while, Sr. Rafqa kept smiling. She was so happy to share in Jesus' Cross, through years of agonizing headaches and nosebleeds and paralysis.

She died with a smile on her face, and everyone who knew her said they loved God more because they had watched Sr. Rafqa love him through her pain.

There will be times when your life is hard. When you have a headache or a stomachache or a heartache, when someone you love is dying or when somebody hurts you. And you have a choice to make then: will you still love God?

Sr. Rafqa shows us that we don't have to love God less when things are hard. In fact, we can love him more. We can take our pain and offer it to Jesus, saying, "Jesus, I love you so much!" And God can use that gift of our pain to make us so holy. He can take that sacrifice and turn it into power, making our prayers even stronger. St. Rafqa Pietra Choboq Ar-Rayès knew how to suffer well, and she can help us all learn the same thing.

St. Rafqa is wearing her Maronite habit and rejoicing in her suffering, her blind eyes closed as she prays her Rosary. She's standing in the valley where her final monastery was situated. The cedar tree is the symbol of Lebanon; these cedars are often mentioned in the Bible and are particularly significant because they were used to build the Temple in Jerusalem. This particular tree is in the shape of the Maronite cross.

Bl. Rani Maria Vattalil

RAH-nee ma-REE-a vut-TAH-lil
India | 1954–1995
Feast Day: February 25

Bl. Rani Maria Vattalil was a sweet little Sister, but the big tough bad guys were awfully scared of her, and just because she wanted to help the poor.

She grew up in a Syro-Malabar Catholic family in a very Catholic part of India. But after she became a Franciscan Clarist Sister, she was sent to northern India, where almost nobody was Catholic.

Sr. Rani Maria started by teaching children, but soon she was working with the poor. She helped them get more money from the men they worked for, men who paid them so little that they were almost starving. She taught them to save money and help each other so they didn't take on terrible debt. She showed them better farming techniques and worked with them so they could send their children to school. The people Sr. Rani Maria helped were amazed at how she loved them.

But not everybody was pleased. Often when people are poor, it's because other people take advantage of them. And there were people who saw Sr. Rani Maria helping the poor and believed she was a threat. Imagine that! A sweet, smiling Sister playing with children and teaching women to save a few dollars a month, and these big, strong men were scared! They told Sr. Rani Maria to stop. They threatened her. But Sr. Rani Maria loved her people and she wasn't willing to abandon them. She kept serving the poor.

So they sent a man to find her on a bus and kill her. Sr. Rani Maria died saying the name of Jesus again and again and her killer went to jail. But Sr. Rani Maria had lived like Jesus, and her family wanted to do the same. So her sister, Sr. Selmy Paul, went to visit Sr. Rani Maria's killer in prison. She forgave him. She even told him she wanted him to be her brother. And after he got out of prison, she took him home to meet her parents, so they could forgive him, too.

Bl. Rani Maria Vattalil didn't shout about Jesus to the people in northern India. She didn't even mention him most of the time. But she lived like Jesus and loved like Jesus and died like Jesus, by serving the lost and the broken, whatever the cost.

Bl. Rani Maria is wearing her Franciscan Clarist habit, with a black veil to show that she was a professed Sister (not a novice) and a knotted cord belt indicating the Sisters' Franciscan charism. She's standing under a canopy in an open air market in the Indian state of Uttar Pradesh and talking with a poor little girl who's carrying her baby brother.

St. Raphael Kalinowski

rahf-ah-YEL kahl-ih-NOF-skee
Lithuania, Poland | 1835–1907
Feast Day: November 15

 Raphael Kalinowski could have been anything he wanted. He was smart and successful and he knew all the right kinds of people. So he tried being a scholar, a soldier, a math professor, a railway engineer, a revolutionary, a prisoner, and a tutor to a prince, Bl. Augustus Czartoryski. But nothing felt quite right.

Raphael tried science first. In college he studied chemistry, zoology, agriculture, and apiculture (which is the study of bees). But even while he studied God's creation, Raphael drifted so far away from God that for years he wasn't going to Mass at all. He ignored the Lord when he was a student, and when he was a math professor too.

But when he was a railway engineer building the tracks that crisscross all of Russia, Raphael had a lot of time to think. He began to wonder about God. Still, he wasn't ready to go to Confession. Luckily for him, Raphael had a sister and a step-mother who loved him very much and loved God even more. They prayed and prayed and eventually convinced Raphael to go to Confession.

And it was a good thing they did! You see, Raphael was living a very dangerous life. He had been a Russian soldier, but he was Polish and he hated to see Russia running his country. So Raphael decid-ed to join the Polish people in rebelling against Russia and became their Minister of War. Which means that when Poland lost the war, Raphael was in huge trouble. He was sentenced to ten years in the salt mines of Siberia.

As it turns out, that's exactly what Raphael needed. There in the silence and the loneliness, he spent all his time with God. Eventually, he was sent to a camp where a priest was also living—it seemed almost miraculous. And God used that time to plant a desire in Raphael's heart. When he was finally free, all he wanted was to be a priest and a religious.

Eventually, Raphael became a Carmelite priest. After over forty years of wandering from one place to another, he finally knew where he belonged and spent the rest of his life serving his people as a priest. St. Raphael Kalinowski could have been anything, but in the end, all he really wanted was to be a saint.

St. Raphael is wearing his Carmelite habit and standing in the doorway to the Carmelite convent at Czerna where he was ordained and where his body is buried. Surrounding him are the many things he sought happiness in before he met Jesus: science books, weapons, railroad-building tools, and even the bees he studied in college.

St. Roque Gonzalez

ROE-kay gohn-SAH-less
Paraguay, Brazil | 1576–1628
Feast Day: November 15

St. Roque Gonzalez was all set to live a fancy life. He was a smart and talented nobleman in Paraguay and he could have become even richer and more powerful and very, very important.

But Roque didn't want any of that. He just wanted Jesus.

So Roque became a Jesuit because those were the men living the simplest life and doing the hardest work. He wanted to work with the poorest people, the ones most likely to be hurt by powerful people. He had grown up speaking both Spanish and Guaraní, the language of the Indigenous people in that part of South America, and now he wanted to serve the Guaraní people. He wanted to tell them about the deep love of Jesus and he wanted to use his name and his power to protect them from wicked men who would try to abuse them or enslave them or rob them of their homes and their culture.

So Fr. Roque helped the Guaraní build settlements where they could be free. Then he lived there with them. He didn't rule over them and he didn't try to make them more like the Spanish. Instead, he helped on their farms and brought them medicine. He got excited about the things they loved: dancing and drums and games. He even asked them to set off fireworks after Mass on big feast days.

He loved them. And they loved him. They trusted him. And because they trusted him, they listened when he talked about Jesus. When other white men had tried to baptize them, the Guaraní had been suspicious. But they knew everything Fr. Roque did was because he loved them. So when he offered to baptize them, they said yes—thousands of them.

Not everybody was pleased with the work Fr. Roque was doing, though. Some of the Guaraní were still suspicious. They thought he had too much power. They didn't like that people were becoming Catholic. So they had him killed, along with two other Jesuit priests. St. Roque Gonzalez had left behind his fancy life to live in poverty and humility, but he ended up with a crown just the same: the crown of martyrdom.

St. Roque is in the rainforest showing an image of the Blessed Mother to two Guaraní children who are wearing simple versions of traditional Guaraní armbands, necklaces, and feathered headdresses. These children lived with Fr. Roque in the reducción (an area reserved for the Indigenous people and protected from slavers). The colors in the picture are inspired by the colors found in ñandutí, a traditional Guaraní lace made by embroidering fabric.

St. Rosalia of Palermo

roe-ZAHL-ee-ah of pah-LAIR-mo
Italy | 1130–1166
Feast Day: September 4

Did you know that the Saints can do even more from heaven than they did on earth? It's because they're alive in heaven, seated at the throne of God. Which means they can pray for us, and sometimes God even works miracles through their prayers.

St. Rosalia of Palermo is a very powerful intercessor. She was a beautiful noble girl living in the king's court in Sicily, but she wasn't interested in all the knights who wanted her to pay attention to them. Rosalia was in love with Jesus and she was *not* going to marry anyone but him.

But while Rosalia was making plans to belong to Jesus, a man named Sir Baldwin was making plans of his own. He had saved the king from a wild animal, and when the king asked him what he wanted as a reward, Baldwin had an answer: "Rosalia's hand in marriage."

The king said yes, but he hadn't asked Rosalia, and when Baldwin proposed she flat out refused. Then, just to be sure, she went home and hacked off all her hair—and not a cute short bob, a crazy, sticking-out-all-over mess. After that, everybody knew she was really serious: she was not going to get married.

But Rosalia knew that people were going to keep trying to change her mind, so she snuck out of the castle and ran away to the mountains. She found a cave and made her home there, foraging in the woods for food and praying for hours and hours every day. And that was the last anybody heard of Rosalia.

Until hundreds of years later, when there was an awful plague in Palermo. When all hope seemed lost, Rosalia appeared to a man whose wife and baby had died of the plague. She told him that if the people of Palermo asked her to pray for them, she would, and the plague would end. People knew that Rosalia had been holy, but nobody had really cared terribly much about her in a very long time. Still, they were willing to try anything. So they begged her to pray and all of a sudden, the plague stopped! They were saved! That's when they realized that even though nobody had much noticed St. Rosalia of Palermo when she was alive, she was a powerful intercessor in heaven—and she still is.

St. Rosalia has just hacked off her hair (which we're told was blonde) and run away to Mount Pellegrino, led by angels to the cave she would then live in. Rosalia is usually pictured holding her skull, since devotion to her is rooted in the miracle wrought when her relics were paraded through Palermo. Instead, we included snapdragons, whose unusual seed pods look like skulls once their flower petals have fallen off.

Bl. Sara Salkaházi

Sara SHAHL-ka-HAH-zee *(ka as in cat)*
Slovakia, Hungary | 1899–1944
Feast Day: December 27

Bl. Sara Salkaházi never quite fit in. When she was a little girl, she was too much of a tomboy. When she got older, she still wasn't ladylike enough, smoking cigarettes and protesting for the rights of workers.

But when she met the Sisters of Social Service, Sara thought she had finally found her place. It didn't matter that she had never wanted to be a Sister—she could change. It didn't matter that she smoked cigarettes—she would find a way to stop. She would do whatever it took; God had called her, and she would go.

But the Sisters weren't so sure. They didn't like the way Sr. Sara acted. They thought she was trying to make everybody pay attention to her, when Sr. Sara was really just trying to help as many people as she could. For a while, the Sisters wouldn't let her take vows with them. They even made her stop wearing their habit for a year. They just weren't sure if they wanted people to look at her and think of them.

But Sr. Sara never gave up. She knew God was calling her there, and she knew he was calling her to be just the way he made her. Oh, she needed to work on her temper. And she was pretty stubborn. But God could purify those things without making her less herself. So she prayed and she worked and finally she took vows as a Sister of Social Service.

It was a lucky thing for the Sisters that she did, too, because Sr. Sara was really holy and a really good worker. She published a magazine and started a college and served the poor and ran a bookstore. And when some very cruel people called Nazis started trying to catch all the Jewish people so they could kill them, Sr. Sara began to hide Jews and teach her Sisters how to do the same. During the war, Sr. Sara saved a hundred Jewish people! Eventually, she was caught and killed, a hero and a martyr.

But she didn't do all those wonderful things because she tried to shrink to be what everyone else expected. No, Bl. Sara Salkaházi's courage and holiness came from being exactly the person God made her to be, even when she didn't quite fit in.

Bl. Sara is wearing the grey habit of the Sisters of Social Service. The Sisters wore a simple habit with a medal of the Holy Spirit and no veil. She's holding a newspaper; she was a journalist in her youth and continued to write even after entering religious life, including many articles attacking Nazi ideology. Sr. Sara is standing in front of the motherhouse of her order in Budapest.

St. Serapion the Sindonite

sah-RAP-ee-uhn the SIN-duh-NITE
Egypt, Greece | d. 356
Feast Day: March 21

If there was an award for Most Generous Man in the World, St. Serapion the Sindonite would have won it. He gave away everything he owned. He even gave away his own self! All because he wanted people to know Jesus.

Some people are sent to preach the Gospel to whole villages and tribes and islands and nations, but Serapion was sent to one person at a time. He had lived for years as a hermit, but God called him to travel to Corinth, a city that was full of sinners. There, Serapion met an actor who didn't know Jesus at all. Serapion wanted to tell him about Jesus, but he knew the man would never listen to him. So what could he do?

He sold himself into slavery.

He gave up his freedom just so he could get close to this man, in the hopes that he would be able to lead the man to Jesus. Once he was the man's slave, Serapion worked really hard, doing all the worst jobs without complaining. The master noticed that Serapion was kind and wise and joyful and finally asked Serapion why he was different. That was Serapion's chance! He got to speak about Jesus at last.

After this, his master was baptized. He was so grateful, he set Serapion free. Only then did Serapion explain that he had become a slave in imitation of Jesus, who made himself a slave to save us.

Then off he went to a new town, where he sold himself into slavery again and gave the money to a poor old widow. Again his master was converted, again Serapion was freed, sent off this time with a coat, a cloak, and a book of the Gospels. But he gave the coat to a beggar and the cloak to an old man, then sold the book to pay a third man's debts. Once again, all he had was his sindon, the strip of fabric he wrapped around himself to stay covered.

It happened again and again. Every time he got something, he gave it away. Every time he was freed, he sold himself again. St. Serapion the Sindonite spent his whole life wandering from town to town, giving himself away for the salvation of souls: the most generous man in the world.

St. Serapion is wearing the sindon he's named for. At his feet are the many things he gave away: money, clothing, even the book of the Gospels. On his right are the pyramids in his homeland of Egypt; on his left, the land of Greece where he gave himself away for the salvation of souls.

Bl. Stanley Rother

Stanley ROE-ther
(th as in thick, not as in then)
United States, Guatemala | 1935–1981
Feast Day: July 28

 Do you ever wonder if God could really use a person as ordinary as you?

Maybe you know that God can do amazing things through ordinary people. Bl. Stanley Rother knew that. Growing up an Oklahoma farm kid who wasn't very good at school, he knew that God could do something wonderful with him—with the great parts of him and the not-so-great parts. So Stanley followed God's call to become a priest. It was hard work getting there. Stanley had a difficult time learning languages, and he was so bad at Latin that he failed out of his first seminary and had to find another.

But eventually Stanley became Fr. Stanley, and soon he was headed to Guatemala to serve the people in Santiago Atitlán. Fr. Stanley was perfect for these farmers living way out in the country. He could help them with their work and teach them new ways to farm. God took Fr. Stanley's gifts and talents and sent him to a people who needed just that.

But Fr. Stanley did *not* have a gift for languages. And while lots of times God uses our nature just as it is to serve his people and make us holy, sometimes he has to work a little miracle in us so we can do his work. Pretty soon, the man who could barely learn Latin had mastered not only Spanish, but also an Indigenous language that not even fifty thousand people can speak! Isn't grace amazing? These people needed a priest who understood them, so God sent them one.

Fr. Stanley loved his people and they loved him. So when the government became suspicious of him, Fr. Stanley didn't want to leave his people, not even to save his life. "The shepherd cannot run," he said, "at the first sign of danger." Even when his bishop called him home to Oklahoma, Fr. Stanley couldn't stop thinking about his people. Like any good priest, he was a father to them, and he missed his children.

So he said goodbye to his family and went back to Guatemala, knowing he would never come home. He was killed there in Guatemala, serving the people he loved. Bl. Stanley Rother, a farm kid from Oklahoma, had let God transform him into a trilingual priest, a martyr, and a witness of God's love.

Bl. Stanley is standing by Lake Atitlán in Santiago Atitlán, Guatemala, with the San Pedro volcano in the background. He's wearing one of the elaborate and colorful stoles that the Tz'utujil people gave him when they accepted him as one of their own after he learned their language. He later established a weaving cooperative so they could sell these beautiful stoles. He's holding a corn seedling, which he attempted to introduce as a cash crop.

Bl. Takayama Ukon

tah-KAH-ya-MAH oo-KOHN
Japan, Philippines | 1552–1615
Feast Day: February 3

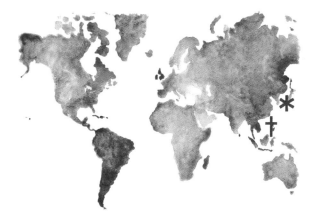

 Takayama Ukon was a samurai lord with a decision to make: would he be a hero, a traitor, or a coward?

Ukon had been baptized when he was eleven, and by the time he was twenty-one he was lord over twenty-five thousand people. He was so kind and spoke so beautifully about Jesus that eighteen thousand of them became Catholic. But Ukon was also a skilled warrior, leading his men so well that the shogun (military dictator) said, "In Ukon's hands a thousand soldiers would be worth more than ten thousand in the hands of anyone else."

But though he had served his emperor well, everyone knew Ukon's real allegiance was to Jesus. And eventually Ukon had to choose: Jesus or Japan.

Well that was no choice at all. Of course he would pick Jesus! But there was still a decision to make. Would he take his thousands of Christian soldiers and march against the emperor? They would die, but they would die in glory!

Ukon wouldn't risk their lives. He wouldn't even risk his own—not because he was scared, but because he knew his people needed him. How could they continue as Christians with nobody to lead them? So Ukon didn't deny his faith as a traitor and he didn't march to his death as a hero. He ran away. Though everyone thought he was a coward, he handed over his castle and his lands. He gave up his reputation as a courageous warrior, not because he was afraid but because his people needed him.

For twenty-six years, the man who had been lord over thousands of souls gave up the honors he deserved and worked instead to preach the Gospel and build churches as a leader but no longer a lord. He wrote poetry and held traditional tea ceremonies, all so he could bring people to Jesus. And when it wasn't enough that he had lost his power and his lands, Ukon went into exile with his wife, his daughter, his grandchildren, and three hundred other Christians who depended on him to lead them. But the journey was too much for him, and Bl. Takayama Ukon died in the Philippines, surrounded by family. To many, he looked like a coward and a weakling, but those who loved him knew that he was really a hero and a martyr.

Bl. Ukon is standing beside a samurai spear and a suit of Yukinoshita armor (which is generally displayed in a seated position). Instead of a sword, he's holding a crucifix; his face shows that he has found peace in leaving behind the life of a samurai warrior to be a soldier of Christ. Ukon's white clothing represents both purity and mourning in Japanese culture, showing that he was holy and prepared to die for Jesus.

St. Teresa Benedicta of the Cross (Edith Stein)

Poland, Germany | 1891–1942
Feast Day: August 9

Edith Stein was one of the most important thinkers of her century. But because she was a woman and because she was Jewish, a lot of people thought she couldn't have anything worthwhile to say.

Edith had grown up in a Jewish family, but by the time she was fourteen she had decided there was no God. This left a pretty big hole in her life, and Edith began to search for answers. She got a PhD in philosophy (the study of wisdom), but she was still searching. Then her Christian friend's husband died and Edith saw the way her friend mourned: she was sad, but not devastated. She knew she would see her husband again in heaven. It was the first time Edith had seen someone changed by the suffering of the Cross and the joy of the resurrection.

Edith began to wonder. Could it possibly be true that Jesus rose from the dead? So Edith did what she always did when she had a question: she grabbed a book. She read and read and read and then went right to a priest to become Catholic.

While all this was going on, Edith was struggling in her job. Even though she was one of the smartest people in Germany, they wouldn't let her be a university professor because she was a woman. That wasn't fair at all! But Edith taught in a women's college instead, until the Nazis came to power. The Nazis hated a lot of people, especially Jewish people. They didn't care that Edith was a Catholic now—she couldn't be a teacher anymore.

Edith knew this was terribly, terribly wrong. Still, she had been hoping to become a Carmelite nun. She had actually tried to leave her teaching job behind before, but the bishop had told her how important her work as a philosopher was. Now she had no choice. She entered the convent, taking the name Sr. Teresa Benedicta of the Cross.

Eventually the Nazis came to find Sr. Teresa Benedicta and take her away. But she was happy to offer her life as a prayer for the Jewish people—her people—that they would all come to know Jesus. As a philosopher, St. Teresa Benedicta of the Cross had spoken brilliantly; as a martyr, she changed the world.

St. Teresa Benedicta is wearing her Carmelite habit with the yellow Star of David that the Nazis forced Jews to wear. She's holding the autobiography of St. Teresa of Avila, the very first Catholic book she read and the one that convinced her she had to study Catholicism. Behind her is Auschwitz concentration camp, where she was killed.

St. Teresa of Calcutta

North Macedonia, India | 1910–1997
Feast Day: September 5

Do you think there are Saints who didn't think prayer was fun? Who didn't always feel wonderful feelings about Jesus? Who sometimes wondered if God really existed?

Absolutely there are! God doesn't ask us to feel feelings, he asks us to choose him, to follow him. And one of the greatest Saints of the twentieth century was a Saint who didn't feel close to Jesus for fifty whole years.

St. Teresa of Calcutta dreamed of being a missionary to India. At eighteen, she became a Sister and worked as a teacher in India for almost twenty years before God called her to found the Missionaries of Charity. Mother Teresa wanted to serve Jesus in what she called "the distressing disguise of the poor," so she put on an Indian sari for a habit and went into the slums to serve. She bathed lepers, combed lice out of orphans' hair, and held people as they died. And she taught the people who joined her to treat each person they met exactly the way they would treat Jesus himself. That's the kind of love everyone deserves.

But the whole time she was working with the poor, Mother Teresa was feeling darkness and emptiness in prayer. It didn't make her turn from God, even though she was working so hard to serve him and getting nothing in return. Her heart was broken, but she kept seeking Jesus. She knew God was with her. She knew she was loved. She just didn't feel it.

Because Mother Teresa felt alone, rejected, and unwanted in prayer, it was easier for her to love people who felt alone, rejected, and unwanted in life. So she thanked God for the darkness. She still loved him. Because love isn't a feeling, love is a choice.

When prayer is hard or when you don't feel loved by God, it's easy to think you're doing something wrong. But then you look at Mother Teresa, who was so good and so holy and prayed so much and did such amazing work for God, and did it all in spiritual darkness. She shows us that holiness isn't about feelings; it's about responding to God's grace and love—even when it doesn't feel good. And now, her darkness is over. In heaven, St. Teresa of Calcutta finally feels God's love again.

St. Teresa is wearing the habit of the Missionaries of Charity, a very simple sari, similar to the one worn by the women who swept the streets at the time Mother Teresa chose it. On the wall behind her are the crucifix and the phrase "I thirst," which are featured in every Missionary of Charity chapel as an invitation to the Sisters to offer their love to Jesus to quench his thirst.

St. Teresa of the Andes

Chile | 1900–1920
Feast Day: April 12

 Teresa of the Andes was pretty and popular and fun—and something of a wild child. She loved to swim, in a pool or in the ocean. She played tennis and croquet, loved singing, played guitar and piano, and was an excellent dancer. When she rode horses (and she loved riding horses), her brother said her wild riding made her look like an Amazon goddess.

Teresa was rich and talented and beautiful. She was also stubborn and vain. She lost her temper easily. One time, she angrily threw out a piece of candy a nun had given her because it wasn't big enough, then bitterly refused a bigger piece—and she was seventeen years old! In short, she wasn't the kind of girl anyone would expect to be a Saint.

But you don't have to be dull to be a Saint. And you don't have to be perfect to be a Saint. To be a Saint, you just have to be the person God made you to be—talents and struggles and all. You just have to fall in love with him and let him make you holy.

That's what Teresa did. From the time she was little, she loved the Virgin Mary and she loved Jesus even more. She realized that there was nothing in the world that was more wonderful than being loved by God. Not parties, not sports, not music. Nothing. And so she began to give her life to him. By God's grace, she fought against her temper and her vanity, and by the time she was fourteen she vowed to belong only to Jesus forever (even if she did still lose her temper sometimes).

At eighteen, Teresa entered a Carmelite monastery. She left behind swimming and horseback riding and dancing, but these sacrifices were nothing compared to the joy of being a Carmelite nun, a bride of Christ. After entering, Sr. Teresa wrote beautiful letters about God's love, but soon got sick. She died before she had been in Carmel for a year.

St. Teresa of the Andes lived a short life that the world would call a waste, but she offered it with no regrets. She had loved deeply and been deeply loved, and all the wealth and beauty and talent of this world can never compare to that. God alone is enough.

St. Teresa is wearing her Carmelite habit and rushing through the courtyard in the Convent of the Holy Spirit in Los Andes, Chile. This courtyard is full of plants and trees for the nuns to enjoy, since they never leave the convent after they enter. Sr. Teresa is holding a crucifix, just as she is in her official Carmelite portrait.

St. Thorlak Thorhallsson

THORE-lack thore-HALL-son
Iceland | 1133–1193
Feast Day: December 23

 Thorlak Thorhallsson was different. He had lots of interesting thoughts, but he didn't like to talk much—except about theology, and then he couldn't stop talking. Today, a lot of people think that maybe Thorlak was autistic, though we can't know for sure.

We do know that Thorlak was very, very smart. He taught himself to read and had memorized all one hundred fifty Psalms before he was even five, then got special permission to be a priest when he was only eighteen years old. After he was ordained he went to France and England to study for six years.

When Fr. Thorlak got back, he realized that things were pretty bad in Iceland. It wasn't that people were treating Christians badly, it's that Christians were behaving badly, especially the priests. Some of them even tried to convince Fr. Thorlak to get married, which was ridiculous because he was already a priest.

It got even harder when he was made bishop. After that, everybody kept crowding him, trying to impress him, asking him questions, looking for favors, and getting frustrated when he didn't act the way they expected. It was exhausting! But God had made him a bishop for a reason. Bishop Thorlak had always had a special gift for understanding God's wisdom and for sharing it with other people. So he began changing things. He made people follow the rules that they'd been ignoring, but he explained why first. In Confession, he gave people very harsh penances, but then he told them he would perform their penance for them. Even when he was being strict, he was merciful.

People weren't always comfortable around Bishop Thorlak. And because they weren't comfortable, they weren't always kind. But Bishop Thorlak was wise and gentle and humble. He had a hard time being with the rich and powerful, but he loved the poor and the sick. And in his twenty years as bishop, he helped reform the Church in Iceland, not by shouting at people but by loving them, teaching them, and calling them back to Jesus.

This wasn't *even though* Bishop Thorlak was different. It was *because* Bishop Thorlak was different. A man who was just like the others wouldn't have been able to do all the good that Bishop Thorlak did. God made St. Thorlak Thorhallsson different, and that's a really good thing.

St. Thorlak is shown in his bishop's vestments, modeled on a medieval Icelandic tapestry that depicted him in colors that were typical of Icelandic textiles. Behind him is a traditional Icelandic turf church, built into the earth with sod and grass up the sides and even covering the roof to keep the congregation warm in the long Icelandic winters. You can see a hint of the northern lights in the sky.

Bl. Vasyl Velychkovsky

VAH-sil VEL-ish-KOHF-skee
Ukraine, Canada | 1903–1973
Feast Day: June 30

othing can destroy the Catholic Church—not Romans, not Ottomans, not atheism, and not communism. Bl. Vasyl Velychkovsky knew this. He knew that the Church had survived in Syrian deserts, in Turkish forests, in English priest-holes, and in Japanese caves. But he didn't expect that the Church might continue to survive through a hotel room consecration—*his* hotel room consecration.

Vasyl was a soldier, then he became a priest in the Ukrainian Greek Catholic Church. He traveled around Ukraine for fifteen years, preaching to hundreds of thousands of people. But when the communists took over, Fr. Vasyl was arrested and sent to Siberia to work in a coal mine, where he built a hidden chapel deep inside a mine shaft and used a spoon for a chalice. After ten years, he was released and returned to Ukraine to lead the underground Church with secret liturgies, secret retreats, and secret seminaries.

Before long, the pope had decided that Fr. Vasyl should become a bishop. There was just one problem: you can only become a bishop if another bishop consecrates you. And all the bishops in Ukraine were in prison. For four years, Fr. Vasyl kept working and wondering: would he ever become a bishop?

Then Fr. Vasyl got a call: could he come to a hotel in Moscow? When he got there, he found a Ukrainian archbishop who had been in prison for eighteen years and had just been released to go to Rome. There, in a Moscow hotel room, with no crowds of excited Catholics, no choir, not even a real altar, he was ordained a bishop. The Church in Ukraine would continue.

Bishop Vasyl served as a bishop for six years and consecrated five secret bishops who could keep the Ukrainian Church going if he was arrested again. And he was. This time, they hurt him terribly and then, when he was nearly dead, told him to leave Ukraine and never come back.

Bl. Vasyl Velychkovsky escaped to Canada, but he only lived in freedom for a year before all that he had suffered in Russia became too much for him. His body gave out, but his life shone as a testament that God will always protect his Church— even if it means making bishops in secret hotel room ceremonies. The gates of hell will not prevail.

Bl. Vasyl is pictured in his own vestments, standing between his salt mine chapel and the apartment that served as his cathedral. He used the lenses of his glasses for a chalice while in prison and the spoon while in the salt mines. Behind him is the cathedral that ought to have been his, St. George's in Lviv. Bishop Vasyl's last arrest was for writing a book about Our Lady of Perpetual Help, whose image hangs in his apartment.

Bl. Victoire Rasoamanarivo

vic-TWAHR rah-SOO-ah-mah-nah-REE-voo
Madagascar | 1848–1894
Feast Day: August 21

It's a good thing Bl. Victoire Rasoamanarivo didn't get her way. That's exactly what God used to save her people.

Victoire was born into a very important family in Madagascar. It was illegal to be a Christian until Victoire was thirteen, but when missionaries came to the country Victoire met some Sisters and soon asked to be baptized. Her family threatened to disown her for it, but Victoire wasn't worried—she knew that the Sisters would let her live with them.

As it turned out, she didn't have to live with the Sisters. But a few years later, when Victoire's parents arranged a marriage for her, she wanted to. She begged the Sisters to let her enter. She didn't want to get married!

But Victoire's family was very powerful—her uncle, the prime minister, was married to the queen. The Sisters pointed out that if Victoire became a Sister, all the Catholics in the country would suffer because of it. Victoire knew they were right. She wanted a vocation to religious life but she didn't have one. So she got married.

It would be lovely to say that Victoire's husband was wonderful and holy, but he wasn't. He wasn't very kind at all. And when he and Victoire weren't able to have children, some people thought Victoire's life was wasted.

But Victoire was a mother to every Catholic in Madagascar. And when all the Catholic missionaries were kicked out, Victoire was left in charge for three years. If she had been a Sister, she might have had to leave. Instead, she taught catechism classes and led the people in prayer and traveled all over the island to remind them who they were: children of God, beloved by the Father. Once, she walked up to an armed soldier who was blocking the door to a church. Fearless, she looked him in the eye and said, "If you must have blood, begin by shedding mine. You can put me to death but you have no right to shut the church." But he couldn't kill the queen's niece! So he opened the church instead.

Eventually, the missionaries came back, but Bl. Victoire Rasoamanarivo didn't fade into the background. She kept working, serving the poor and teaching the young and reminding everybody that God's plan is always better than ours.

Bl. Victoire is wrapped in a striped lamba, a traditional piece of fabric often worn as a shawl or sarong; it's also used to carry babies and to wrap the bodies of the dead for a funeral. Victoire's rosary never left her hands as it was her favorite prayer. The book represents her role as catechist and the lemur reminds us of the ninety percent of plant and animal species in Madagascar that are endemic to the island.

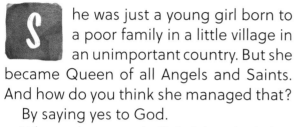

Palestine
Feast Day: January 1

She was just a young girl born to a poor family in a little village in an unimportant country. But she became Queen of all Angels and Saints. And how do you think she managed that?

By saying yes to God.

When the angel Gabriel asked her if she would be the Mother of God, the Blessed Virgin Mary didn't have to wonder and worry—she said yes. And when she had to travel to Bethlehem and give birth in a stable, she knew that was God asking her to do his will. So she said yes, without fussing or pouting or wishing she had a more comfortable bed. Mary knew that saying yes to God meant trying to rejoice in his will, even if she didn't always understand it.

She said yes when the shepherds came, yes when the magi came. And every night, as they fled through the desert to Egypt, Mary said yes to God again. She didn't demand that God fix the mess they were in and she didn't complain about how hard things were, she just loved God and loved everybody around her.

Mary didn't only say yes to God in big things. For years, saying yes to God just meant making dinner and changing diapers, telling stories and kissing scraped knees. But eventually, it meant giving up her Son. Mary said yes to God when she watched Jesus walk away from her, ready to begin his ministry. She said yes when she watched him suffer, when she heard her Son tell her to be mother to us all. And when she watched him die, when she hugged his risen body, when she taught and loved the apostles after Jesus had ascended into heaven—Mary was always saying yes to God.

Finally, God brought her body and soul home to heaven because he loved her so much. But (because he loves *us* so much) Mary is still hard at work saying yes to God—appearing to children like St. Jacinta Marto, to ladies like St. Mariam Baouardy, to men like St. Juan Diego. Every time, she's asking her children to do what she did: to know how much God loves us and to say yes to him, whatever he asks. That's how an ordinary child becomes a king or a queen.

The Blessed Mother is shown here as the Ark of the Covenant, the center of God's presence in the Old Testament. Like the Ark, she's covered in gold and draped in fabric of blue, purple, and scarlet. Her crown has stars (from her heavenly coronation) and almond blossoms (like the Ark's lampstand). Baby Jesus is holding the flowering almond rod of Aaron the high priest, the staff of Aaron's authority that is held in the Ark.

Geographical Index

Bl. Pier Giorgio Frassati (166), St. Rosalia of Palermo (180)

Lithuania: St. Raphael Kalinowski (176)

Montenegro: St. Leopold Mandić (112)

Netherlands: Bl. Peter Donders (158)

North Macedonia: St. Teresa of Calcutta (192)

Poland: St. Albert Chmielowski (8), Bl. Emilian Kovch (58), St. Faustina Kowalska (64), Bl. Ladislaus Bukowinski (104), St. Raphael Kalinowski (176), St. Teresa Benedicta of the Cross/Edith Stein (190)

Portugal: St. Jacinta Marto (76)

Russia: Bl. Laurentia Herasymiv (108), Bl. Leonid Feodorov (110), St. Olga of Kiev (148)

Scotland: St. Columba of Iona (40)

Slovakia: Bl. Sara Salkáhazi (182)

Slovenia: St. Jerome (80)

Spain: St. Casilda of Toledo (30), Bl. Ceferino Giménez Malla (34), St. Eulalia of Mérida (62), St. Pedro de San José Betancur (154)

Sweden: St. Elizabeth Hesselblad (56)

Switzerland: St. Adelaide of Burgundy (4)

Ukraine: Bl. Emilian Kovch (58), Bl. Laurentia Herasymiv (108), St. Olga of Kiev (148), Bl. Vasyl Velychkovsky (198)

MIDDLE EAST

Iran: St. James Intercisus (78)

Lebanon: St. Rafqa Pietra Choboq Ar-Rayès (172)

Palestine: St. Jerome (80), St. Mariam Baouardy (128), Virgin Mary (202)

Syria: St. Ephrem the Syrian (60)

Turkey: St. Ephrem the Syrian (60), St. Macrina the Younger (116), St. Pulcheria (168)

NORTH AMERICA

Canada: St. André Bessette (14), Bl. Dina Bélanger (52), St. Kateri Tekakwitha (98), Bl. Vasyl Velychkovsky (198)

Costa Rica: Bl. María Romero Meneses (124)

El Salvador: St. Oscar Romero (150)

Guatemala: St. Pedro de San José Betancur (154), Bl. Stanley Rother (186)

Mexico: Bl. Concepción Cabrera de Armida (42), St. Juan Diego Cuauhtlatoatzin (94), St. Rafael Guízar y Valencia (170)

Nicaragua: Bl. María Romero Meneses (124)

Puerto Rico: Bl. Carlos Manuel Rodríguez Santiago (28)

United States: St. Damien of Molokai (46), St. Kateri Tekakwitha (98), St. Katharine Drexel (100), Bl. Stanley Rother (186)

OCEANIA

Australia: St. Mary MacKillop (136)

Papua New Guinea: Bl. Peter To Rot (162)

SOUTH AMERICA

Argentina: Bl. Ceferino Namuncurá (36), Bl. María Antonia de Paz y Figueroa (122)

Brazil: St. Dulce Pontes (54), Bl. Francisca de Paula de Jesus (66), St. Roque Gonzalez (178),

Chile: St. Teresa of the Andes (194)

Colombia: St. Laura Montoya (106)

Paraguay: St. Roque Gonzalez (178)

Peru: Bl. Ana of the Angels Monteagudo (12), St. Martin de Porres (134)

Suriname: Bl. Peter Donders (158)

Feast Day Index

August 13: St. Dulce Pontes (54)

August 21: Bl. Victoire Rasoamanarivo (200)

August 26: Bl. Ceferino Namuncurá (36)

August 26: Bl. Laurentia Herasymiv (108)

August 26: St. Mariam Baouardy (128)

August 27: St. Monica (138)

August 28: St. Moses the Strong (140)

September 4: Bl. Dina Bélanger (52)

September 4: St. Rosalia of Palermo (180)

September 5: St. Teresa of Calcutta (192)

September 10: St. Pulcheria (168)

September 17: St. Hildegard of Bingen (74)

September 18: Bls. Daudi Okelo and Jildo Irwa (48)

September 20: Sts. Augustine Yu Chin-gil, Peter Yu Tae-chol (18)

September 25: Bl. Hermann of Reichenau (72)

September 28: St. Lorenzo Ruiz (114)

September 30: St. Jerome (80)

October 5: St. Faustina Kowalska (64)

October 9: St. John Henry Newman (86)

October 12: Bl. Carlo Acutis (26)

October 17: St. John Colobus (84)

October 21: St. Laura Montoya (106)

November 3: St. Martin de Porres (134)

November 7: St. Peter Wu Guosheng (164)

November 15: St. Raphael Kalinowski (176)

November 15: St. Roque Gonzalez (178)

November 24: Sts. Augustine Phan Viết Huy, Dominic Đinh Đạt, and Nicholas Bùi Đức Thể (16)

November 27: St. James Intercisus (78)

November 29: Bl. Denis of the Nativity (50)

December 1: Bl. Marie-Clémentine Anuarite Nengapeta (130)

December 5: Bl. Nicolas Steno (144)

December 9: St. Juan Diego Cuauhtlatoatzin (94)

December 10: St. Eulalia of Mérida (62)

December 16: St. Adelaide of Burgundy (4)

December 16: Bl. Paul Thoj Xyooj (152)

December 23: St. Thorlak Thorhallsson (196)

December 25: St. Albert Chmielowski (8)

December 25: Bl. Maria Therese von Wüllenweber (126)

December 26: Bl. Cecilia Butsi Wongwai (32)

December 27: Bl. Sara Salkaházi (182)

Topical Index

Chronological Index

Bl. Leonid Feodorov (110), St. Leopold Mandić (112), Bl. María Romero Meneses (124), Bl. Marie-Clémentine Anuarite Nengapeta (130), Bl. Nicholas Bunkerd Kitbamrung (142), Bl. Oscar Romero (150), Bl. Paul Thoj Xyooj (152), Bl. Peter To Rot (162), Bl. Pier Giorgio Frassati (166), St. Rafael Guízar y Valencia (170), Bl. Rani Maria Vattalil (174), Bl. Sara Salkaházi (182), Bl. Stanley Rother (186), St. Teresa Benedicta of the Cross/St. Edith Stein (190), St. Teresa of Calcutta (192), St. Teresa of the Andes (194), Bl. Vasyl Velychkovsky (198)
Twenty-First Century: Bl. Carlo Acutis (26)